The Rate of Return on Everything

1870–2015

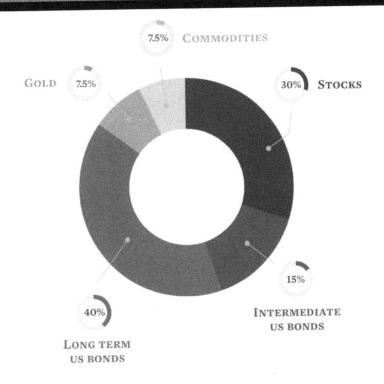

Federal Reserve Bank of San Francisco

stanfordpub.com

The Rate of Return on Everything, 1870–2015

Òscar Jordà
Federal Reserve Bank of San Francisco
University of California, Davis

Katharina Knoll
Deutsche Bundesbank

Dmitry Kuvshinov
University of Bonn

Moritz Schularick
University of Bonn and CEPR

Alan M. Taylor
University of California, Davis
NBER and CEPR

December 2017

_____

Suggested citation:

Jordà, Òscar, Katharina Knoll, Dmitry Kuvshinov, Moritz Schularick, Alan M. Taylor. 2017. "The Rate of Return on Everything, 1870–2015" Federal Reserve Bank of San Francisco Working Paper 2017-25. _____

The Rate of Return on Everything, 1870–2015[*]

Òscar Jordà[†]   Katharina Knoll[‡]   Dmitry Kuvshinov[§]

Moritz Schularick[¶]   Alan M. Taylor[✠]

November 2017

Abstract

This paper answers fundamental questions that have preoccupied modern economic thought since the 18th century. What is the aggregate real rate of return in the economy? Is it higher than the growth rate of the economy and, if so, by how much? Is there a tendency for returns to fall in the long-run? Which particular assets have the highest long-run returns? We answer these questions on the basis of a new and comprehensive dataset for all major asset classes, including—for the first time—total returns to the largest, but oft ignored, component of household wealth, housing. The annual data on total returns for equity, housing, bonds, and bills cover 16 advanced economies from 1870 to 2015, and our new evidence reveals many new insights and puzzles.

Keywords: return on capital, interest rates, yields, dividends, rents, capital gains, risk premiums, household wealth, housing markets.

JEL classification codes: D31, E44, E10, G10, G12, N10.

[*]This work is part of a larger project kindly supported by research grants from the Bundesministerium für Bildung und Forschung (BMBF) and the Institute for New Economic Thinking. We are indebted to a large number of researchers who helped with data on individual countries. We are especially grateful to Francisco Amaral for outstanding research assistance, and would also like to thank Felix Rhiel, Mario Richarz, Thomas Schwarz and Lucie Stoppok for research assistance on large parts of the project. For their helpful comments we thank Roger Farmer, Philipp Hofflin, David Le Bris, Emi Nakamura, Thomas Piketty, Matthew Rognlie, Jón Steinsson, Clara Martínez-Toledano Toledano, Stijn Van Nieuwerburgh, and conference participants at the NBER Summer Institute EFG Program Meeting and the Bank of England. All errors are our own. The views expressed herein are solely the responsibility of the authors and should not be interpreted as reflecting the views of the Federal Reserve Bank of San Francisco, the Board of Governors of the Federal Reserve System or the Deutsche Bundesbank.

[†]Federal Reserve Bank of San Francisco; and Department of Economics, University of California, Davis (oscar.jorda@sf.frb.org; ojorda@ucdavis.edu).

[‡]Deutsche Bundesbank (katharina.knoll@bundesbank.de).

[§]Department of Economics, University of Bonn (dmitry.kuvshinov@uni-bonn.de).

[¶]Department of Economics, University of Bonn; and CEPR (moritz.schularick@uni-bonn.de).

[✠]Department of Economics and Graduate School of Management, University of California, Davis; NBER; and CEPR (amtaylor@ucdavis.edu).

1. INTRODUCTION

What is the rate of return in an economy? This important question is as old as the economics profession itself. David Ricardo and John Stuart Mill devoted much of their time to the study of interest and profits, while Karl Marx famously built his political economy in *Das Kapital* on the idea that the profit rate tends to fall over time. Today, in our most fundamental economic theories, the real risk-adjusted returns on different asset classes reflect equilibrium resource allocations given society's investment and consumption choices over time. Yet much more can be said beyond this observation. Current debates on inequality, secular stagnation, risk premiums, and the natural rate, to name a few, are all informed by conjectures about the trends and cycles in rates of return.

For all the abundance of theorizing, however, evidence has remained scant. Keen as we are to empirically evaluate many of these theories and hypotheses, to do so with precision and reliability obviously requires long spans of data. Our paper introduces, for the first time, a large annual dataset on total rates of return on all major asset classes in the advanced economies since 1870—including for the first-time total returns to the largest but oft ignored component of household wealth, housing. Housing wealth is on average roughly one half of national wealth in a typical economy, and can fluctuate significantly over time (Piketty, 2014) . But there is no previous rate of return database which contains any information on housing returns. Here we build on prior work on house prices (Knoll, Schularick, and Steger, 2017) and new data on rents (Knoll, 2016) to offer an augmented database to track returns on this very important component of the national capital stock.

Thus, our first main contribution is to document our new and extensive data collection effort in the main text and in far more detail in an extensive companion appendix.

We have painstakingly compiled annual asset return data for 16 advanced countries, over nearly 150 years. We construct three types of returns: investment income (i.e., yield), capital gains (i.e., price changes), and total returns (i.e., the sum of the two). These calculations were done for four major asset classes, two of them risky—equities and housing—and two of them relatively safe—government bonds and bills. Along the way, we have also brought in auxiliary sources to validate our data externally. Our data consist of actual asset returns taken from market data. In that regard, our data are therefore more detailed than returns inferred from wealth estimates in discrete benchmark years as in Piketty (2014). We also follow earlier work in documenting annual equity, bond, and bill returns, but here again we have taken the project further. We re-compute all these measures from original sources, improve the links across some important historical market discontinuities (e.g., closures and other gaps associated with wars and political instability), and in a number of cases we access new and previously unused raw data sources. Our work thus provides researchers with the first non-commercial database of historical equity, bond, and bill returns, with the most extensive coverage across both countries and years, and the evidence drawn from our data will establish new foundations for long-run macro-financial research.

Indeed, our second main contribution is to uncover fresh and unexpected stylized facts which bear on active research debates, showing how our data offer fertile ground for future enquiry.

1

In one contentious area of research, the accumulation of capital, the expansion of capital's share in income, and the growth rate of the economy relative to the rate of return on capital all feature centrally in the current debate sparked by (Piketty, 2014) on the evolution of wealth, income, and inequality. What do the long-run patterns on the rates of return on different asset classes have to say about these possible drivers of inequality?

Another strand of research, triggered by the financial crisis and with roots in Alvin Hansen's (1939) AEA Presidential Address, seeks to revive the secular stagnation hypothesis (Summers, 2014). Demographic trends are pushing the world's economies into uncharted territory. We are living longer and healthier lives and spending more time in retirement. The relative weight of borrowers and savers is changing and with it the possibility increases that the interest rate will fall by an insufficient amount to balance saving and investment at full employment. Are we now, or soon to be, in the grip of another period of secular stagnation?

In a third major strand of financial research, preferences over current versus future consumption, and attitudes toward risk, manifest themselves in the premiums that the rates of return on risky assets carry over safe assets. A voluminous literature followed the seminal work of Mehra and Prescott (1985). Returns on different asset classes, their volatilities, their correlations with consumption, and with each other, sit at the core of the canonical consumption-Euler equation that underpins asset pricing theories, and more broadly, the demand side of an aggregate economy in all standard macro models. But tensions remain between theory and data, prompting further explorations of new asset pricing paradigms including behavioral finance. Our new data adds another risky asset class to the mix, housing. Along with equities, and when compared against the returns on bills and bonds, can our new data provide new tests to compare and contrast alternative paradigms, some of which depend on rarely observed events that require samples over long spans of time?

Lastly, in the sphere of monetary economics, Holston, Laubach, and Williams (2017) show that estimates of the natural rate of interest in several advanced economies have gradually declined over the past four decades and are now near zero. As a result, the probability that the nominal policy interest rate may be constrained by the effective lower bound has increased, raising questions about the prevailing policy framework. In this regard, how frequent and persistent are such downturns in the natural rate and could there be a need for our monetary policy frameworks to be revised?

The common thread running through each of these broad research topics is the notion that the rate of return is central to understanding long-, medium-, and short-run economic fluctuations. But which rate of return? And how do we measure it? The risky rate is a measure of profitability of private investment. The safe rate plays an important role in benchmarking compensation for risk, and is often tied to discussions of monetary policy settings and the notion of the natural rate.

Our paper follows a long and venerable tradition of economic thinking about fundamental returns on capital that includes, among others, Adam Smith, Knut Wicksell, and John Maynard Keynes. More specifically, our paper is closely related, and effectively aims to bridge the gap, between two literatures. The first is rooted in finance and is concerned with long-run returns on different assets. The literature on historical asset price returns and financial markets is too large to discuss in detail, but important contributions have been made with recent digitization of historical financial time series, such as the project led by William Goetzmann and Geert Rouwenhorst at Yale's International Center for Finance. The book *Triumph of the Optimists* by Dimson, Marsh, and Staunton (2009) probably marked the first comprehensive attempt to document and analyze long-run returns on investment for a broad cross-section of countries. Another key contribution to note is the pioneering and multi-decade project to document the history of interest rates by Homer and Sylla (2005).

The second related strand of literature is the analysis of comparative national balance sheets over time, as in Goldsmith (1985). More recently, Piketty and Zucman (2014) have brought together data from national accounts and other sources tracking the development of national wealth over long time periods. They also calculate rates of return on capital by dividing aggregate capital income the national accounts by the aggregate value of capital, also from national accounts. Our work is both complementary and supplementary to theirs. It is complementary as the asset price perspective and the national accounts approach are ultimately tied together by accounting rules and identities. Using market valuations, we are able to corroborate and improve the estimates of returns on capital that matter for wealth inequality dynamics. Our long-run return data are also supplementary to the work of Piketty and Zucman (2014) in the sense that we quadruple the number of countries for which we can calculate real rates of return, enhancing the generality of our findings.

Major findings   We summarize our four main findings as follows.

1. **On risky returns,** r_{risky} Until this paper, we have had no way to know rates of return on all risky assets in the long run. Research could only focus on the available data on equity markets (Campbell, 2003; Mehra and Prescott, 1985). We uncover several new stylized facts.

    In terms of total returns, residential real estate and equities have shown very similar and high real total gains, on average about 7% per year. Housing outperformed equity before WW2. Since WW2, equities have outperformed housing on average, but only at the cost of much higher volatility and higher synchronicity with the business cycle. The observation that housing returns are similar to equity returns, yet considerably less volatile, is puzzling. Diversification with real estate is admittedly harder than with equities. Aggregate numbers do obscure this fact although accounting for variability in house prices at the local level still appears to leave a great deal of this housing puzzle unresolved.

    Before WW2, the real returns on housing and equities (and safe assets) followed remarkably similar trajectories. After WW2 this was no longer the case, and across countries equities then experienced more frequent and correlated booms and busts. The low covariance of equity and housing returns reveals significant aggregate diversification gains (i.e., for a representative agent) from holding the two asset classes. Absent the data introduced in this paper, economists had been unable to quantify these gains.

3

One could add yet another layer to this discussion, this time by considering international diversification. It is not just that housing returns seem to be higher on a rough, risk-adjusted basis. It is that, while equity returns have become increasingly correlated across countries over time (specially since WW2), housing returns have remained uncorrelated. Again, international diversification may be even harder to achieve than at the national level. But the thought experiment suggests that the ideal investor would like to hold an internationally diversified portfolio of real estate holdings, even more so than equities.

2. **On safe returns,** r_{safe} We find that the real safe asset return has been very volatile over the long-run, more so than one might expect, and oftentimes even more volatile than real risky returns. Each of the world wars was (unsurprisingly) a moment of very low safe rates, well below zero. So was the 1970s inflation and growth crisis. The peaks in the real safe rate took place at the start of our sample, in the interwar period, and during the mid-1980s fight against inflation. In fact, the long decline observed in the past few decades is reminiscent of the decline that took place from 1870 to WW1. Viewed from a long-run perspective, it may be fair to characterize the real safe rate as normally fluctuating around the levels that we see today, so that today's level is *not* so unusual. Consequently, we think the puzzle may well be why was the safe rate so high in the mid-1980s rather than why has it declined ever since.

Safe returns have been low on average, falling in the 1%–3% range for most countries and peacetime periods. While this combination of low returns and high volatility has offered a relatively poor risk-return trade-off to investors, the low returns have also eased the pressure on government finances, in particular allowing for a rapid debt reduction in the aftermath of WW2.

How do the trends we expose inform current debates on secular stagnation and economic policy more generally? International evidence in Holston, Laubach, and Williams (2017) on the decline of the natural rate of interest since the mid-1980s is consistent with our richer cross-country sample. This observation is compatible with the secular stagnation hypothesis, whereby the economy can fall into low investment traps (see, for example Summers, 2014) and Eggertsson and Mehrotra (2014). More immediately, the possibility that advanced economies are entering an era of low real rates calls into question standard monetary policy frameworks based on an inflation target. Monetary policy based on inflation targeting had been credited for the Great Moderation, until the Global Financial Crisis. Since that turbulent period, the prospect of long stretches constrained by the effective lower bound have commentators wondering whether inflation targeting regimes are the still the right approach for central banks (Williams, 2016).

3. **On the risk premium,** $r_{risky} - r_{safe}$ Over the very long run, the risk premium has been volatile. A vast literature in finance has typically focused on business-cycle comovements in short span data (see, for example Cochrane, 2009, 2011). Yet our data uncover substantial

swings in the risk premium at lower frequencies that sometimes endured for decades, and which far exceed the amplitudes of business-cycle swings.

In most peacetime eras this premium has been stable at about 4%–5%. But risk premiums stayed curiously and persistently high from the 1950s to the 1970s, persisting long after the conclusion of WW2. However, there is no visible long-run trend, and mean reversion appears strong. Curiously, the bursts of the risk premium in the wartime and interwar years were mostly a phenomenon of collapsing safe rates rather than dramatic spikes in risky rates.

In fact, the risky rate has often been smoother and more stable than safe rates, averaging about 6%–8% across all eras. Recently, with safe rates low and falling, the risk premium has widened due to a parallel but smaller decline in risky rates. But these shifts keep the two rates of return close to their normal historical range. Whether due to shifts in risk aversion or other phenomena, the fact that safe rates seem to absorb almost all of these adjustments seems like a puzzle in need of further exploration and explanation.

4. **On returns minus growth,** $r_{wealth} - g$ Turning to real returns on all investable wealth, Piketty (2014) argued that, if the return to capital exceeded the rate of economic growth, rentiers would accumulate wealth at a faster rate and thus worsen wealth inequality. Comparing returns to growth, or "r minus g" in Piketty's notation, we uncover a striking finding. Even calculated from more granular asset price returns data, the same fact reported in Piketty (2014) holds true for more countries and more years, and more dramatically: namely "$r \gg g$."

In fact, the only exceptions to that rule happen in very special periods: the years in or right around wartime. In peacetime, r has always been much greater than g. In the pre-WW2 period, this gap was on average 5% per annum (excluding WW1). As of today, this gap is still quite large, in the range of 3%–4%, and it narrowed to 2% during the 1970s oil crises before widening in the years leading up to the Global Financial Crisis.

However, one puzzle that emerges from our analysis is that while "r minus g" fluctuates over time, it does not seem to do so systematically with the growth rate of the economy. This feature of the data poses a conundrum for the battling views of factor income, distribution, and substitution in the ongoing debate (Rognlie, 2015). Further to this, the fact that returns to wealth have remained fairly high and stable while aggregate wealth increased rapidly since the 1970s, suggests that capital accumulation may have contributed to the decline in the labor share of income over the recent decades (Karabarbounis and Neiman, 2014). In thinking about inequality and several other characteristics of modern economies, the new data on the return to capital that we present here should spur further research.

2. A NEW HISTORICAL GLOBAL RETURNS DATABASE

The dataset unveiled in this study covers nominal and real returns on bills, bonds, equities, and residential real estate in 16 countries from 1870 to 2015. The countries covered are Australia, Belgium, Denmark, Finland, France, Germany, Italy, Japan, the Netherlands, Norway, Portugal, Spain, Sweden, Switzerland, the United Kingdom, and the United States. Table 1 summarizes the data coverage by country and asset class.

In this section, we will discuss the main sources and definitions for the calculation of long-run returns. A major innovation is the inclusion of housing. Residential real estate is the main asset in most household portfolios, as we shall see, but so far very little has been known about long-run returns on housing.

Like most of the literature, we examine returns to national aggregate holdings of each asset class. Theoretically, these are the returns that would accrue for the hypothetical representative-agent investor holding each country's portfolio. Within country heterogeneity is undoubtedly important, but clearly beyond the scope of a study covering nearly 150 years of data and 16 advanced economies.

Table 1: *Data coverage*

Country	Bills	Bonds	Equities	Housing
Australia	1870–2015	1900–2015	1870–2015	1901–2015
Belgium	1870–2015	1870–2015	1870–2015	1890–2015
Denmark	1875–2015	1870–2015	1893–2015	1876–2015
Finland	1870–2015	1870–2015	1896–2015	1920–2015
France	1870–2015	1870–2015	1870–2015	1871–2015
Germany	1870–2015	1870–2015	1870–2015	1871–2015
Italy	1870–2015	1870–2015	1870–2015	1928–2015
Japan	1876–2015	1881–2015	1886–2015	1931–2015
Netherlands	1870–2015	1870–2015	1900–2015	1871–2015
Norway	1870–2015	1870–2015	1881–2015	1871–2015
Portugal	1880–2015	1871–2015	1871–2015	1948–2015
Spain	1870–2015	1900–2015	1900–2015	1901–2015
Sweden	1870–2015	1871–2015	1871–2015	1883–2015
Switzerland	1870–2015	1900–2015	1900–2015	1902–2015
UK	1870–2015	1870–2015	1871–2015	1900–2015
USA	1870–2015	1871–2015	1872–2015	1891–2015

2.1. The composition of wealth

Table 2 and Figure 1 show the decomposition of economy-wide investable asset holdings and capital stock average shares across five major economies at the end of 2015: France, Germany, Japan, UK and USA. Investable assets, displayed on the left panel of Figure 1, exclude assets that relate to intra-financial holdings and cannot be held directly by investors, such as loans, derivatives (apart from employee stock options), financial institutions' deposits, insurance and pension claims.[1] That leaves housing, other non-financial assets—mainly other buildings, machinery, and equipment—equity, bonds, bills, deposits and other financial assets, which mainly include private debt securities (corporate bonds and asset-backed securities). The right panel of Figure 1 shows the decomposition of the capital stock into housing and various other non-financial assets. The decomposition of investable assets into individual classes for each country, is further shown in Table 2.

Housing, equity, bonds, and bills comprise over half of all investable assets in the advanced economies today (nearly two-thirds whenever deposit rates are added). The housing returns data also allow us to assess returns on around half of the outstanding total capital stock, using our new total return series as a proxy for aggregate housing returns. Our improved and extended equity return data for publicly-traded equities will then be used, as is standard, as a proxy for aggregate business equity returns.[2]

2.2. Historical return data

Our measure of the bill return, the canonical risk-free rate, is taken to be the yield on Treasury bills, i.e., short-term, fixed-income government securities. The yield data come from the latest vintage of the long-run macrohistory database (Jordà, Schularick, and Taylor, 2016b).[3] For periods when data on Treasury bill returns were unavailable, we relied on either money market rates or deposit rates of banks from Zimmermann (2017).

Our measure of the bond return is taken to be the the total return on long-term government bonds. Unlike a number of preceding cross-country studies, we focus on the bonds listed and traded on local exchanges, and denominated in local currency. The focus on local-exchange bonds makes the bond return estimates more comparable to those of equities, housing and bills. Further, this results in a larger sample of bonds, and focuses our attention on those bonds that are more likely to be held by the representative household in the respective country. For some countries and periods we have made use of listings on major global exchanges to fill gaps where domestic markets were thin, or local exchange data were not available (for example, Australian bonds listed in New York or

---

[1] Both decompositions also exclude human capital, which cannot be bought or sold. Lustig, Van Nieuwerburgh, and Verdelhan (2013) show that for a broader measure of aggregate wealth that includes human capital, the size of human wealth is larger than of non-human wealth, and its return dynamics are similar to those of a long-term bond.

[2] For example, to proxy the market value of unlisted equities, the US Financial Accounts apply industry-specific stock market valuations to the net worth and revenue of unlisted companies.

[3] www.macrohistory.net/data

Table 2: *Composition of investable assets by country*

Country	Housing	Equity	Bonds	Bills	Deposits	Other financial	Other non-financial
France	23.2	28.0	5.1	1.5	10.4	11.9	19.8
Germany	22.2	24.2	5.6	0.2	14.0	17.3	16.4
Japan	10.9	13.4	13.1	1.5	18.9	12.9	29.4
UK	27.5	24.8	6.1	0.2	10.7	12.6	18.1
USA	13.3	39.1	8.6	0.8	7.3	11.2	19.8
Average share	19.4	25.9	7.7	0.9	12.3	13.2	20.7

Note: Ratios to total investable assets, percentage points. End-2015. Data are sourced from national accounts and national wealth estimates published by the countries' central banks and statistical offices.

Figure 1: *Composition of investable assets and capital stock in the major economies*

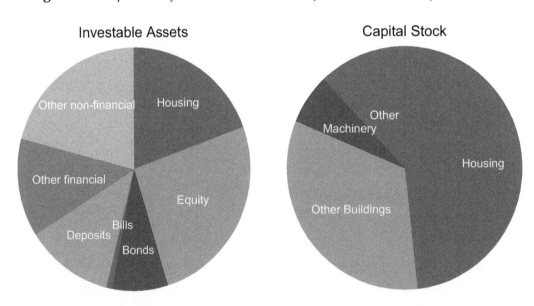

Note: Composition of total investable assets and capital stock. Average of the individual asset shares of France, Germany, Japan, UK and US, end-2015. Investable assets are defined as the gross total of economy-wide assets excluding loans, derivatives, financial institutions' deposits, insurance, and pension claims. The capital stock is business capital plus housing. Data are sourced from national accounts and national wealth estimates published by the countries' central banks and statistical offices.

London). Throughout the sample we target a maturity of around 10 years. For the second half of the 20th century, the maturity of government bonds is generally accurately defined. For the pre-WW2 period we sometimes had to rely on data for perpetuals, i.e., very long-term government securities (such as the British consol).

Our dataset also tracks the development of returns on equity and housing. The new data on total returns on equity come from a broad range of sources, including articles in economic and financial history journals, yearbooks of statistical offices and central banks, stock exchange listings, newspapers, and company reports. Throughout most of the sample, we rely on indices weighted by market capitalization of individual stocks, and a stock selection that is representative of the entire stock market. For some historical time periods in individual countries, however, we also make use of indices weighted by company book capital, stock market transactions, or weighted equally, due to limited data availability.

To the best of the authors' knowledge, this study is the first to present long-run returns on residential real estate. We combine the long-run house price series presented by Knoll, Schularick, and Steger (2017) with a novel dataset on rents from Knoll (2016). For most countries, the rent series rely on the rent components of the cost of living of consumer price indices as constructed by national statistical offices and combine them with information from other sources to create long-run series reaching back to the late 19th century.

We also study a number of "composite" asset returns, as well as those on the individual asset classes—bills, bonds, equities and housing—described above. More precisely, we compute the rate of return on safe assets, risky assets, and aggregate wealth, as weighted averages of the individual asset returns. To obtain a representative return from the investor's perspective, we use the outstanding stocks of the respective asset in a given country as weights. To this end, we make use of new data on equity market capitalization (from Kuvshinov and Zimmermann, 2017) and housing wealth for each country and period in our sample, and combine them with existing estimates of public debt stocks to obtain the weights for the individual assets. A graphical representation of these asset portfolios, and further description of their construction is provided in the Appendix Section E.

Tables A.14 and A.15 present an overview of our four asset return series by country, their main characteristics and coverage. The paper comes with an extensive data appendix that specifies the sources we consulted and discusses the construction of the series in greater detail (see the Data Appendix, Section K for housing returns, and Section L for equity and bond returns).

2.3. Calculating returns

The total annual return on any financial asset can be divided into two components: the capital gain from the change in the asset price P, and a yield component Y, that reflects the cash-flow return on an investment. The total nominal return R for asset i in country j at time t is calculated as:

$$\text{Total return:} \quad R_{i,j,t} = \frac{P_{i,j,t} - P_{i,j,t-1}}{P_{i,j,t-1}} + Y_{i,j,t}. \tag{1}$$

Because of wide differences in inflation across time and countries, it is helpful to compare returns in real terms. Let $\pi_{j,t} = (CPI_{i,j,t} - CPI_{i,j,t-1})/CPI_{i,j,t-1}$ be the realized consumer price index (*CPI*) inflation rate in a given country j and year t. We calculate inflation-adjusted *real returns r* for each asset class as

$$\text{Real return:} \quad r_{i,j,t} = (1 + R_{i,j,t})/(1 + \pi_{j,t}) - 1. \tag{2}$$

These returns will be summarized in period average form, by country, or for all countries.[4]

Investors must be compensated for risk to invest in risky assets. A measure of this "excess return" can be calculated by comparing the real total return on the risky asset with the return on a risk-free benchmark—in our case, the government bill rate, $r_{bill,j,t}$. We therefore calculate the excess return *ER* for the risky asset i in country j as

$$\text{Excess return:} \quad ER_{i,j,t} = r_{i,j,t} - r_{bill,j,t}. \tag{3}$$

In addition to individual asset returns, we also present a number of weighted "composite" returns aimed at capturing broader trends in risky and safe investments, as well as the "overall return" or "return on wealth." Appendix E provides further details on the estimates of country asset portfolios from which we derive country-year specific weights.

For safe assets, we assume that total public debt is divided equally into bonds and bills to proxy the bond and bill stocks, since we have no data yet on the market weights (only total public debt weight) over our full sample. The safe asset return is then computed as an average of the real returns on bonds and bills as follows:

$$\text{Safe return:} \quad r_{safe,j,t} = \frac{r_{bill,j,t} + r_{bond,j,t}}{2}. \tag{4}$$

For risky assets, the weights w here are the asset holdings of equity and housing stocks in the respective country j and year t, scaled to add to 1. We use stock market capitalization and housing wealth as weights for equity and housing. The risky asset return is a weighted average of returns on equity and housing:

$$\text{Risky return:} \quad r_{risky,j,t} = r_{equity,j,t} \times w_{equity,j,t} + r_{housing,t} \times w_{housing,j,t}. \tag{5}$$

The difference between our risky and safe return measures then provides a proxy for the aggregate risk premium in the economy:

$$\text{Risk premium:} \quad RP_{j,t} = r_{risky,j,t} - r_{safe,j,t}. \tag{6}$$

---

[4]In what follows we focus on conventional average annual real returns. In addition, we often report period-average geometric mean returns corresponding to the annualized return that would be achieved through reinvestment or compounding. These are calculated as $\left(\prod_{i \in T}(1 + r_{i,j,t})\right)^{\frac{1}{T}} - 1$. Note that the arithmetic period-average return is always larger than the geometric period-average return, with the difference increasing with the volatility of the sequence of returns.

The "return on wealth" measure is a weighted average of returns on risky assets (equity and housing) and safe assets (bonds and bills). The weights w here are the asset holdings of risky and safe assets in the respective country j and year t, scaled to add to 1.

$$\text{Return on wealth:} \quad r_{wealth,j,t} = r_{risky,j,t} \times w_{risky,j,t} + r_{safe,t} \times w_{safe,j,t}. \tag{7}$$

For comparison, Appendix Section F also provides information on the equally-weighted risky return, and the equally-weighted rate of return on wealth, that are simple averages of housing and equity, and housing, equity and bonds respectively.

Finally, we also consider returns from a global investor perspective in Appendix Section G. These measure the returns from investing in local markets in US dollars. This measure effectively subtracts the depreciation of the local exchange rate vis-a-vis the dollar from the nominal return:

$$\text{USD return:} \quad R_{i,j,t}^{USD} = R_{i,j,t} - \Delta s_{j,t}, \tag{8}$$

where $\Delta s_{j,t}$ is the depreciation of the local exchange rate vis-a-vis the US dollar in year t

The real USD returns are then computed net of US inflation $\pi_{USA,t}$:

$$\text{Real USD return:} \quad r_{i,j,t}^{USD} = (1 + R_{i,j,t}^{USD})/(1 + \pi_{USA,t}) - 1, \tag{9}$$

2.4. Constructing housing returns using the rent-price approach

This section briefly describes our methodology to calculate total housing returns, and we provide further details as needed later in the paper (Section 6.2 and Appendix Section K).

We construct estimates for total returns on housing using the rent-price approach. This approach starts from a benchmark rent-price ratio (RI_0/HPI_0) estimated in a baseline year ($t = 0$). For this ratio we rely on net rental yields the Investment Property Database (IPD).[5][6] We can then construct a time series of returns by combining separate information from a country-specific house price index series (HPI_t/HPI_0) and a country-specific rent index series (RI_t/RI_0). For these indices we rely on prior work on housing prices (Knoll, Schularick, and Steger, 2017) and new data on rents (Knoll, 2016). This method assumes that the indices cover a representative portfolio of houses. If so, there is no need to correct for changes in the housing stock, and only information about the growth rates in prices and rents is necessary.

---

[5]Net rental yields use rental income net of maintenance costs, ground rent and other irrecoverable expenditure. We use net rather than gross yields to improve comparability with other asset classes.

[6]For Australia, we use the net rent-price ratio from Fox and Tulip (2014). For Belgium, we construct a gross rent-price ratio using data from Numbeo.com, and scale it down to account for running costs and depreciation. Both of these measures are more conservative than IPD, and more in line with the alternative benchmarks for these two countries.

Given the above, a time series of the rent-to-price ratio can be derived iteratively as

$$\frac{RI_{t+1}}{HPI_{t+1}} = \left[\frac{(RI_{t+1}/RI_t)}{(HPI_{t+1}/HPI_t)}\right]\frac{RI_t}{HPI_t}. \tag{10}$$

In a second step, returns on housing can be computed as:

$$R_{house,t+1} = \frac{RI_{t+1}}{HPI_t} + \frac{HPI_{t+1} - HPI_t}{HPI_t}. \tag{11}$$

As this approach is sensitive to the choice of rent-price-ratio at benchmark dates, we corroborate the plausibility of the historical rent-price ratios with additional primary sources as well as economic and financial history books and articles. Where the rent-price approach estimates diverge from the alternative historical sources, we additionally benchmark the ratio to historical estimates of net rental yields. We also examine the sensitivity of aggregate return estimates to varying benchmark ratio assumptions. For further details, see Section 6.2 and Appendix Section K.

3. RATES OF RETURN: AGGREGATE TRENDS

We begin with the first key finding—one that was completely unknown until now, due to lack of evidence. The data summary in Table 3 and Figure 2 show that residential real estate, not equity, has been the best long-run investment over the course of modern history. The full sample summary return data are shown in the upper panel of Table 3, and the post-1950 sample in the bottom panel. Data are pooled and equally-weighted, i.e., they are raw rather than portfolio returns. We include wars so that results are not polluted by omitted disasters. We do, however, exclude hyperinflations in order to focus on the underlying trends in returns, rather than inflation.

Although returns on housing and equities are similar, the volatility of housing returns is substantially lower, as Table 3 shows. Returns on the two asset classes are in the same ballpark—around 7%—but the standard deviation of housing returns is substantially smaller than that of equities (10% for housing versus 22% for equities). Predictably, with thinner tails, the compounded return (using the geometric average) is vastly better for housing than for equities—6.6% for housing versus 4.6% for equities. This finding appears to contradict one of the basic assumptions of modern valuation models: higher risks should come with higher rewards.

We can see that differences in asset returns are not driven by unusual events in the early pre-WW2 part of our long historical sample. The bottom half of Table 3 makes this point. Compared to the full sample period (1870–2015) reported in the upper half of the table, the same clear pattern emerges: stocks and real estate dominate in terms of returns. Moreover, average returns post–1950 are similar to the full sample, even though the later period excludes the devastating effects of the two world wars.

Other robustness checks are reported in the Appendix in Figures A.1, A.2, and A.3. Briefly, we find that the observed patterns are not driven by the smaller European countries in our sample.

Table 3: *Global real returns*

	Real returns				Nominal Returns			
	Bills	Bonds	Equity	Housing	Bills	Bonds	Equity	Housing
Full sample:								
Mean return p.a.	0.98	2.50	6.89	7.05	4.60	6.10	10.75	11.06
Std.dev.	6.01	10.74	21.94	9.98	3.33	8.91	22.78	10.70
Geometric mean	0.78	1.94	4.64	6.61	4.55	5.74	8.55	10.59
Mean excess return p.a.	.	1.53	5.91	6.07				
Std.dev.	.	8.38	21.43	9.86				
Geometric mean	.	1.19	3.81	5.64				
Observations	1739	1739	1739	1739	1739	1739	1739	1739
Post-1950:								
Mean return p.a.	0.87	2.77	8.28	7.44	5.40	7.31	12.99	12.31
Std.dev.	3.43	9.94	24.20	8.88	4.04	9.80	25.09	10.15
Geometric mean	0.81	2.30	5.54	7.10	5.33	6.89	10.28	11.90
Mean excess return p.a.	.	1.91	7.41	6.57				
Std.dev.	.	9.20	23.77	9.19				
Geometric mean	.	1.51	4.79	6.21				
Observations	1016	1016	1016	1016	1016	1016	1016	1016

Note: Annual global returns in 16 countries, equally weighted. Period coverage differs across countries. Consistent coverage within countries. Excess returns are computed relative to bills.

Figure 2: *Global real rates of return*

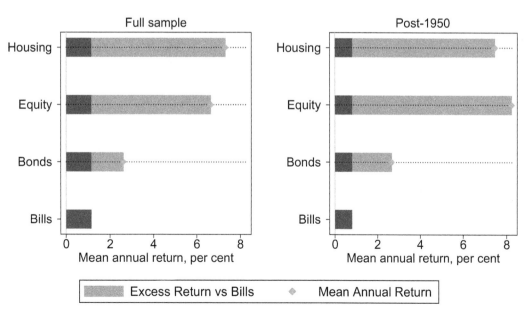

Notes: Arithmetic avg. real returns p.a., unweighted, 16 countries. Consistent coverage within each country.

Figure A.1 shows average real returns weighted by country-level real GDP, both for the full sample and post–1950 period. Compared to the unweighted averages, equity performs slightly better, but the returns on equity and housing remain very similar, and the returns and riskiness of all four asset classes are very close to the unweighted series in Table 3.

The results could be biased because different countries enter the sample at different dates due to data availability. Figure A.2 plots the average returns for sample-consistent country groups, starting at benchmark years—the later the benchmark year, the more countries we can include. Again, the broad patterns discussed above are largely unaffected.

We also investigate the possibility that the results are biased because of wartime experiences. We recompute average returns, but now dropping the two world wars from the sample. Figure A.3 plots the average returns in this case, and alas the main result remains largely unchanged. Appendix Table A.3 also considers the risky returns during wartime in more detail, to assess the evidence for rare disasters in our sample. Returns during both wars were indeed low and often negative, although returns during World War 2 in a number of countries were relatively robust.

Finally, our aggregate return data take the perspective of a domestic investor in a representative country. Appendix Table A.9 instead takes the perspective of a global US-Dollar investor, and assesses the US-Dollar value of the corresponding returns. The magnitude and ranking of returns are similar to those in Table 3 above, although the volatilities are substantially higher, as expected given that the underlying asset volatility is compounded by that in the exchange rate. This higher volatility is also reflected in somewhat higher levels of US-Dollar returns, compared to those in local currency.

4. SAFE RATES OF RETURN

Figure 3 shows the trends in real returns on government bonds (solid line) and bills (dashed line) since 1870. The global returns are GDP-weighted averages of the 16 countries in our sample. Although we do not show the unweighted data, the corresponding figure would look very similar. We smooth the data using a decadal moving average—for example, the observation reported in 1900 is the average of data from 1895 to 1905.

Two striking features of Figure 3 deserve comment. First, we can see that low real rates, and in fact negative real rates have been relatively common during modern financial history. Second, for the most part returns to long-term and short-term safe assets have tracked each other very closely—with a premium of about 1% that has widened considerably since the well-documented decline of the mid-1980s (Holston, Laubach, and Williams, 2017).

Safe rates are far from stable in the medium-term. There is enormous time series, as well as cross-country variability. In fact, real safe rates appear to be as volatile (or even more volatile) than real risky rates, a topic we return to in the next subsection. Considerable variation in the risk premium often comes from sharp changes in safe real rates, not from the real returns on risky assets.

Two four-decade-long declines in real rates stand out: (1) from 1870 to WW1 (with a subsequent

14

Figure 3: *Trends in real returns on bonds and bills*

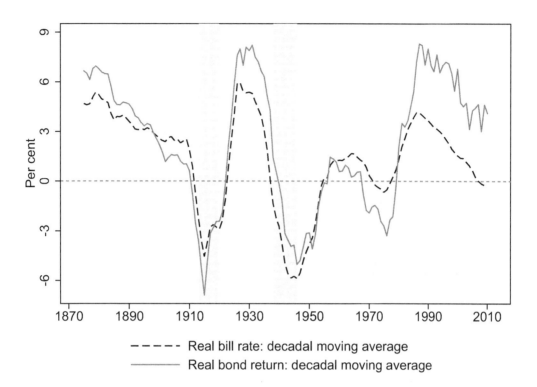

- - - - - Real bill rate: decadal moving average
———— Real bond return: decadal moving average

Note: Mean returns for 16 countries, weighted by real GDP. Decadal moving averages.

further collapse during the war); and (2) the well-documented decline that started in the mid-1980s. Add to this list the briefer, albeit more dramatic decline that followed the Great Depression into WW2. Some observers have therefore interpreted the recent downward trend in safe rates as a sign of "secular stagnation" (see, for example Summers, 2014).

However, in contrast to 1870 and the late 1930s, the more recent decline is characterized by a much higher term premium—a feature with few precedents in our sample. There are other periods in which real rates remained low, such as in the 1960s. They were pushed below zero, particularly for the longer tenor bonds, during the 1970s inflation spike, although here too term premiums remained relatively tight. Returns dip dramatically during both world wars. It is perhaps to be expected: demand for safe assets spikes during disasters although the dip may also reflect periods of financial repression that usually emerge during times of conflict, and which often persist into peacetime. Thus, from a broad historical perspective, high rates of return on safe assets and high term premiums are more the exception than the rule.

Summing up, during the late 19th and 20th century, real returns on safe assets have been low—on average 1% for bills and 2.5% for bonds—relative to alternative investments. Although the return volatility—measured as annual standard deviation—is lower than that of housing and equities, these assets offered little protection during high-inflation eras and during the two world wars, both periods of low consumption growth.

Figure 4: *Correlations across safe asset returns*

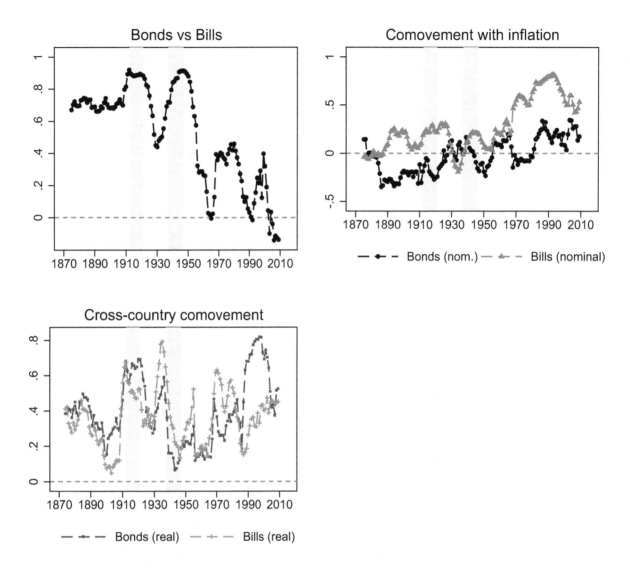

Note: Rolling decadal correlations. The global correlation coefficient is the average of individual countries for the rolling window. Cross-country correlation coefficient is the average of all country pairs for a given asset class. Country coverage differs across time periods.

Figure 4 explores additional key moments of the data. The top-left panel plots the correlation between real bond and bill returns, again using decadal rolling windows and computed as the cross-sectional average of correlations. In parallel to our discussion of the term premium, real returns on bonds and bills have been highly correlated for most of the sample up until the 1960s. From the 1970s onwards, the era of fiat money and higher average inflation, this correlation has become much weaker, and near zero at times, coinciding with a widening term premium.

The top right panel of Figure 4 displays the correlation between nominal safe asset returns and inflation. The figure shows that safe assets provided more of an inflation hedge starting in the 1970s, around the start of the era of modern central banking. However, as Figure 3 showed, both

Table 4: *Real rates of return on bonds and bills*

Country	Full Sample		Post 1950		Post 1980	
	Bills	Bonds	Bills	Bonds	Bills	Bonds
Australia	1.29	2.24	1.32	2.45	3.23	5.85
Belgium	1.16	3.01	1.50	3.86	2.30	6.24
Denmark	3.08	3.58	2.18	3.50	2.80	7.13
Finland	0.64	3.22	0.63	4.86	2.61	5.76
France	-0.47	1.54	0.95	2.96	2.22	6.94
Germany	1.51	3.15	1.86	3.69	1.96	4.22
Italy	1.20	2.53	1.30	2.83	2.42	5.85
Japan	0.68	2.54	1.36	2.83	1.48	4.53
Netherlands	1.37	2.71	1.04	2.14	2.08	5.59
Norway	1.10	2.55	-0.26	1.94	1.50	5.62
Portugal	-0.01	2.23	-0.65	1.59	0.65	6.25
Spain	-0.04	1.41	-0.32	1.21	2.20	5.72
Sweden	1.77	3.25	0.82	2.70	1.51	6.59
Switzerland	0.89	2.41	0.12	2.33	0.33	3.35
UK	1.16	2.29	1.14	2.63	2.70	6.67
USA	2.17	2.79	1.30	2.64	1.71	5.71
Average, unweighted	1.13	2.61	0.89	2.76	1.98	5.75
Average, weighted	1.31	2.49	1.17	2.65	1.89	5.55

Note: Average annual real returns. Period coverage differs across countries. Consistent coverage within countries. The average, unweighted and average, weighted figures are respectively the unweighted and real-GDP-weighted arithmetic averages of individual country returns.

bonds and bills have experienced prolonged periods of negative real returns—both during wartime inflation, and the high-inflation period of the late 1970s. Although safe asset rates usually comove positively with inflation, they do not always compensate the investor fully.

The bottom panel of Figure 4 displays the cross correlation of safe returns over rolling decadal windows to examine how much inflation risk can be diversified with debt instruments. This correlation coefficient is the average of all country-pair combinations for a given window, and is calculated as

$$Corr_{i,t} = \frac{\sum_j \sum_{k \neq j} Corr(r_{i,j,t \in T}, r_{i,k,t \in T})}{\sum_j \sum_{k \neq j} 1}$$

for asset i (here: bonds or bills), and time window $T = (t-5, t+5)$. Here j and k denote the country pairs, and r denotes real returns, constructed as described in Section 2.3.

Cross-country real safe returns have exhibited positive comovement throughout history. The degree of comovement shows a few marked increases associated with WW1 and the 1930s. The effect of these major global shocks on individual countries seems to have resulted in a higher correlation of cross-country asset returns. This was less true of WW2 and its aftermath, perhaps because the evolving machinery of financial repression was better able to manage the yield curve.

Turning to cross-sectional features, Table 4 shows country-specific safe asset returns for three

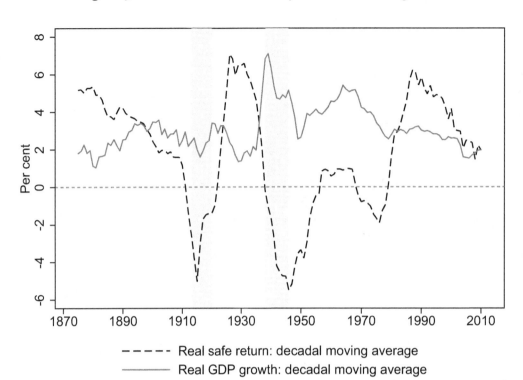

Figure 5: *Trends in real return on safe assets and GDP growth*

- - - - - Real safe return: decadal moving average
———— Real GDP growth: decadal moving average

Note: Mean returns and GDP growth for 16 countries, weighted by real GDP. Decadal moving averages. The safe rate of return is an arithmetic average of bonds and bills.

samples: all years, post–1950, and post–1980. Here the experiences of a few countries stand out. In France, real bill returns have been negative when averaged over the full sample. In Portugal and Spain, they have been approximately zero. In Norway, the average return on bills has been negative for the post-1950 sample. However, most other countries have experienced reasonably similar returns on safe assets, in the ballpark of $1\% - 3\%$.

Aside from the investor perspective discussed above, safe rates of return have important implications for government finances, as they measure the cost of raising and servicing government debt. What matters for this is not the level of real return *per se*, but its comparison to real GDP growth, or $r_{safe} - g$. If the rate of return exceeds real GDP growth, $r_{safe} > g$, reducing the debt/GDP ratio requires continuous budget surpluses. When r_{safe} is less than g, however, a reduction in debt/GDP is possible even with the government running modest deficits.

Figure 5 plots the representative "safe rate of return"—the arithmetic average of bond and bill returns (dashed line)—against real GDP growth (solid line), again as decadal moving averages. Starting in the late 19th century, safe rates were higher than GDP growth, meaning that any government wishing to reduce debt had to run persistent budget surpluses. Indeed, this was the strategy adopted by Britain to pay off the debt incurred during the Napoleonic War (Crafts, 2016). The two world wars saw low real returns, but nevertheless a large debt accumulation to finance the wartime effort. The aftermath of these two wars, however, offered vastly different experiences for public finances. After World War 1, safe returns were high and growth—low, requiring significant budgetary efforts to repay the war debts. This was particularly difficult given the additional reparations imposed by the Treaty of Versailles, and the turbulent macroeconomic environment at the time. After World War 2, on the contrary, high growth and inflation helped greatly reduce the value of national debt, creating $r_{safe} - g$ gaps as large as –10 percentage points.

More recently, the Great Moderation saw a reduction in inflation rates and a corresponding increase in the debt financing burden, whereas the impact of $r_{safe} - g$ in the aftermath of the Global Financial Crisis remains broadly neutral, with the two rates roughly equal. On average throughout our sample, the real growth rate has been around 1 percentage point higher than the safe rate of return (3% growth versus 2% safe rate), meaning that governments could run small deficits without increasing the public debt burden.

In sum, real returns on safe assets, even adjusted for risk, have been quite low across the advanced countries and throughout the last 150 years. In fact, for some countries, these returns have been persistently negative. Periods of unexpected inflation, in war and peace, have often diluted returns, and flights to safety have arguably depressed returns in the asset class even further in the more turbulent periods of global financial history. The low return for investors has, on the flipside, implied a low financing cost for governments, which was particularly important in reducing the debts incurred during World War 2.

5. RISKY RATES OF RETURN

We next shift our focus to look at the risky assets in our portfolio, i.e., housing and equities. Figure 6 shows the trends in real returns on housing (solid line) and equity (dashed line) for our entire sample, again presented as decadal moving averages. In addition, Figure 7 displays the correlation of risky returns between asset classes, across countries, and with inflation, in a manner similar to Figure 4.

A major stylized fact leaps out. Prior to WW2, real returns on housing, safe assets and equities followed remarkably similar trajectories. After WW2 this was no longer the case. Risky returns were high and stable in the 19th century, but fell sharply around WW1, with the decade-average real equity returns turning negative. Returns recovered quickly during the 1920s, before experiencing a reasonably modest drop in the aftermath the Great Depression. Most strikingly though, from the onset of WW2 onwards the trajectories of the two risky asset classes diverged markedly from each other, and also from those of safe assets.

Equity returns have experienced many pronounced global boom-bust cycles, much more so than housing returns, with real returns as high as 16% and as low as −4% over the course of entire decades. Equity returns fell in WW2, boomed sharply during the post-war reconstruction, and fell off again in the climate of general macroeconomic instability in the late 1970s. Equity returns bounced back following a wave of deregulation and privatization of the 1980s. The next major event to consider was the Global Financial Crisis, which extracted its toll on equities and to some extent

Figure 6: *Trends in real returns on equity and housing*

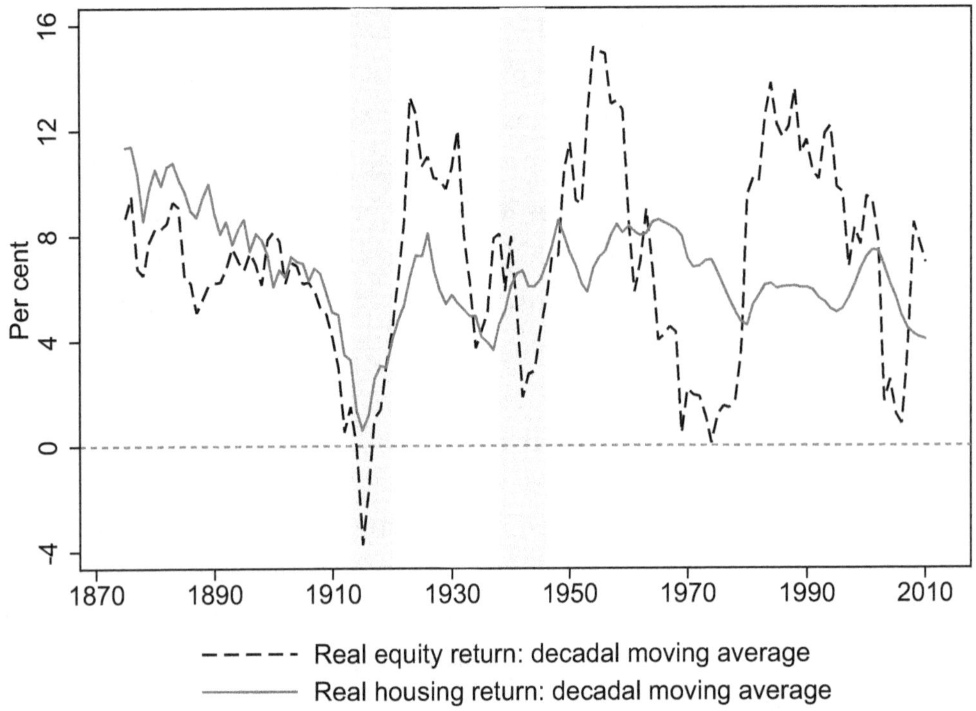

Note: Mean returns for 16 countries, weighted by real GDP. Decadal moving averages.

housing, as we shall see.

Housing returns, on the other hand, have remained remarkably stable over the entire post-WW2 period. As a consequence, the correlation between equity and housing returns, depicted in the top panel of Figure 7, was highly positive before WW2, but has all but disappeared over the past five decades. The low covariance of equity and housing returns over the long run reveals attractive gains from diversification across these two asset classes that economists, up to now, have been unable to measure or analyze.

In terms of relative returns, housing persistently outperformed equity up until the end of WW1, even though the returns followed a broadly similar temporal pattern. In recent decades, equities have slightly outperformed housing on average, but only at the cost of much higher volatility and cyclicality. Furthermore, the upswings in equity prices have generally not coincided with times of low growth or high inflation, when standard theory would say high returns would have been particularly valuable.

The top-right panel of Figure 7 shows that equity co-moved negatively with inflation in the 1970s, while housing provided a more robust hedge against rising consumer prices. In fact, apart from the interwar period when the world was gripped by a general deflationary bias, equity returns have co-moved negatively with inflation in almost all eras. Moreover, the big downswings in equity returns in the two world wars and the 1970s coincided with periods of generally poor economic

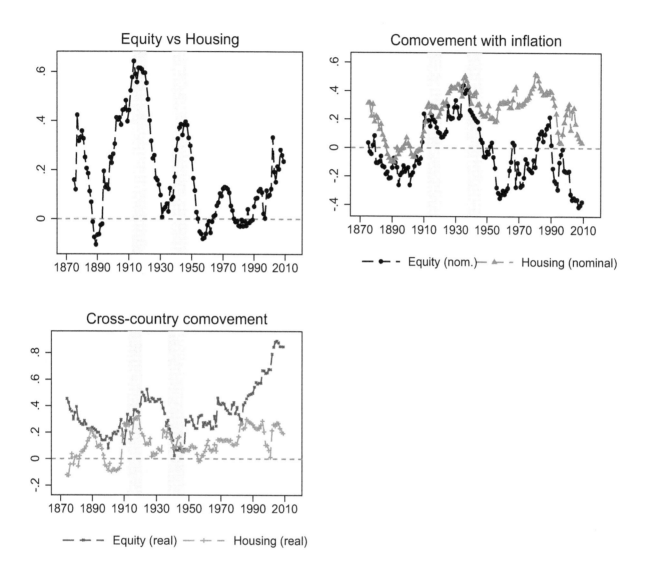

Figure 7: *Correlations across risky asset returns*

Note: Rolling decadal correlations. The global correlation coefficient is the average of individual countries for the rolling window. Cross-country correlation coefficient is the average of all country pairs for a given asset class. Country coverage differs across time periods.

performance.

In the past two decades, equity returns have also become highly correlated across countries, as shown by the sharp rise in the degree of comovement in the bottom-left panel of Figure 7. A well-diversified global equity portfolio has become less of a hedge against country-specific risk (Quinn and Voth, 2008). As is a matter of debate, this may reflect the greater trading across equity markets globally, or an increase in the global shocks to which firms, especially those in the typical equity index, are increasingly exposed. In contrast to equities, cross-country housing returns have remained relatively uncorrelated, perhaps because housing assets remain less globally tradable than equities or are exposed more to idiosyncratic country-level shocks.

Table 5: *Real rates of return on equity and housing*

Country	Full Sample		Post 1950		Post 1980	
	Equity	Housing	Equity	Housing	Equity	Housing
Australia	7.81	6.37	7.57	8.29	8.78	7.16
Belgium	6.23	7.89	9.65	8.14	11.49	7.20
Denmark	7.22	8.10	9.33	7.04	12.57	5.14
Finland	9.98	9.58	12.81	11.18	16.17	9.47
France	3.25	6.54	6.38	10.38	11.07	6.39
Germany	6.85	7.82	7.52	5.29	10.06	4.12
Italy	7.32	4.77	6.18	5.55	9.45	4.57
Japan	6.09	6.54	6.32	6.74	5.79	3.58
Netherlands	7.09	7.28	9.41	8.53	11.90	6.41
Norway	5.95	8.03	7.08	9.10	11.76	9.81
Portugal	4.37	6.31	4.70	6.01	8.34	7.15
Spain	5.46	5.21	7.11	5.83	11.00	4.62
Sweden	7.98	8.30	11.30	8.94	15.74	9.00
Switzerland	6.71	5.63	8.73	5.64	10.06	6.19
UK	7.20	5.36	9.22	6.57	9.34	6.81
USA	8.39	6.03	8.75	5.62	9.09	5.66
Average, unweighted	6.60	7.25	8.24	7.46	10.68	6.42
Average, weighted	7.04	6.69	8.13	6.34	8.98	5.39

Note: Average annual real returns. Period coverage differs across countries. Consistent coverage within countries. The average, unweighted and average, weighted figures are respectively the unweighted and real-GDP-weighted arithmetic averages of individual country returns.

Next we explore long-run risky returns in individual countries. Table 5 shows the returns on equities and housing by country for the full sample and for the post–1950 and post–1980 subsamples. Long-run risky asset returns for most countries are close to 6%–8% per year, a figure which we think represents a robust and strong real return to risky capital.

Still, the figures also show an important degree of heterogeneity among individual countries. Many of the countries that have experienced large political shocks show lower equity returns. This is the case for Portugal and Spain which both underwent prolonged civil strife, and France which undertook a wave of nationalizations in the aftermath of WW2. French equity returns are also negatively affected by the fallout from the world wars, and the fallout from an oil crisis in the 1960s (for more detail, see Blancheton, Bonin, and Le Bris, 2014; Le Bris and Hautcoeur, 2010). In contrast, real equity returns in Finland have been as high as 10%, on average throughout the sample. Housing returns also show considerable heterogeneity. Returns on housing have been high on average in the Nordic countries, but low in Italy and Spain. The US risky asset returns fall roughly in the middle of the country-specific figures, with equity returns slightly above average, and housing returns—slightly below. Our estimates of the US housing returns are in line with those in Favilukis, Ludvigson, and Van Nieuwerburgh (2017).[7] The degree of heterogeneity and the relative ranking of

---

[7]Favilukis, Ludvigson, and Van Nieuwerburgh (2017) estimate a gross nominal return on US housing of 9%—11%, based on three data sources going back to 1950s and 1970s. This implies a net real return of around 5—7% (once inflation, maintenance and running costs are subtracted), in line with our estimates in Table 5.

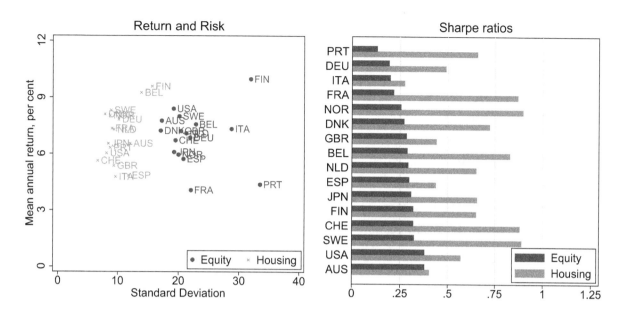

Figure 8: *Risk and return of equity and housing*

Note: Left panel: average real return p.a. and standard deviation. Right panel: Sharpe ratios, measured as $(\bar{r}_i - \bar{r}_{bill})/\sigma_i$, where i is the risky asset with $\bar{r}_i$ mean return and σ_i standard deviation. 16 countries. Consistent coverage within each country.

returns is broadly similar when comparing the full sample to the post-1950 period.

This country-level evidence reinforces one of our main findings: housing has been as good a long-run investment as equities, and possibly better. Housing has offered a similar return to equity in the majority of countries and time periods. In the long-run, housing outperformed equities in absolute terms in 6 countries, and equities outperformed housing in 5. Returns on the two assets were about the same in the remaining 5 countries. After WW2, housing was the best-performing asset class in 3 countries, and equities in 9.

However, although aggregate returns on equities exceed aggregate returns on housing for certain countries and time periods, equities do not outperform housing in simple risk-adjusted terms. Figure 8 compares the riskiness and returns of housing and equities for each country. The left panel plots average annual real returns on housing (orange crosses) and equities (green circles) against their standard deviation. The right panel shows the Sharpe ratios for equities (in dark green) and housing (in orange) for each country in the sample.[8] Housing provides a higher return per unit of risk in each of the 16 countries in our sample, with Sharpe ratios on average more than double those of equities.

---

[8]The Sharpe ratio is calculated as $(\bar{r}_i - \bar{r}_{bill})/\sigma_i$, where i is the risky asset (housing or equity) with $\bar{r}_i$ mean return and σ_i standard deviation.

5.1. Decomposition of returns

What explains the superior risk-adjusted performance of housing relative to equities? To gain insights into this question, we separately analyze movements in capital gains and income yield as shown in Tables 6 and 7. The table shows both arithmetic and geometric average world returns over the entire sample and since 1950. Capital gain measures the return from price appreciation only. Depending on the asset, other components of total returns measure income from either dividends or rents received by the investor. Both capital gain and dividend or rental income are expressed as a proportion of the previous period's price. The small residual between combined capital gain and dividend income, and the equity total return, accounts for gain and loss from capital operations such as stock splits or share buybacks, and income from reinvestment of dividends.

Table 6 shows that the main reason risk-adjusted housing returns are higher is the lower volatility of house prices. Both rental yields and dividend income are relatively stable for all years and countries throughout the sample. However, the standard deviation of equity prices is double that of house prices over the full sample, and around 2.5 times that of house prices after 1950.

Equity prices have experienced large swings and high-amplitude cycles throughout the course of modern history. Moreover, capital gains—the more volatile component—are responsible for a larger share of equity total returns than they are for housing. These two factors have become even more relevant during the post-WW2 decades.

A similar pattern is visible at the country level, with the summary statistics shown in Table 7.

Table 6: *Total nominal return components for equity and housing.*

		Full Sample		Post 1950	
		Arithmetic	Geometric	Arithmetic	Geometric
Housing	Capital gain	5.72 (10.42)	5.25	7.22 (9.82)	6.82
	Rental income	5.49 (2.02)	5.47	5.26 (1.92)	5.24
	Total return	11.22 (10.76)	10.73	12.47 (10.23)	12.05
	Capital gain share	51%	49%	58%	57%
Equity	Capital gain	6.62 (22.17)	4.46	9.17 (24.64)	6.47
	Dividend income	4.18 (1.80)	4.16	3.81 (1.89)	3.79
	Total return	10.81 (22.67)	8.63	13.00 (25.30)	10.24
	Capital gain share	61%	52%	71%	63%
	Observations	1675	1675	985	985

Note: Average annual nominal returns across 16 countries, unweighted. Standard deviation in parentheses. Period coverage differs across countries. Consistent coverage within countries.

Table 7: *Total nominal return components for equity and housing by country.*

	Housing				Equity				Obs.
	Capital gain	Rental income	Total return	Capital gain share	Capital gain	Dividend income	Total return	Capital gain share	
Australia	6.53	4.03	10.56	61.85%	7.09	4.92	12.01	59.04%	113
	(13.72)	(0.89)	(13.81)		(16.70)	(1.08)	(17.36)		
Belgium	5.78	6.15	11.93	48.46%	6.84	3.83	10.67	64.11%	115
	(10.09)	(1.46)	(9.94)		(23.73)	(1.64)	(24.35)		
Denmark	4.95	6.90	11.85	41.80%	6.15	4.85	11.01	55.91%	123
	(7.93)	(2.49)	(8.11)		(18.04)	(2.24)	(18.50)		
Finland	8.72	7.19	15.91	54.82%	10.30	5.09	15.37	67.00%	91
	(14.70)	(2.89)	(15.74)		(31.19)	(1.98)	(31.80)		
France	7.49	5.25	12.73	58.80%	4.86	3.74	8.60	56.54%	136
	(9.28)	(0.99)	(9.73)		(20.93)	(1.34)	(21.27)		
Germany	3.50	6.03	9.52	36.73%	4.33	3.88	8.45	51.31%	111
	(10.20)	(2.61)	(10.85)		(21.32)	(1.60)	(21.97)		
Italy	7.29	3.49	10.77	67.63%	9.28	3.61	12.89	71.99%	81
	(14.74)	(1.59)	(15.03)		(31.23)	(1.30)	(31.48)		
Japan	5.89	4.70	10.60	55.60%	6.82	2.68	9.88	69.05%	70
	(9.60)	(1.24)	(9.97)		(18.51)	(1.76)	(18.88)		
Netherlands	5.25	5.96	11.21	46.86%	7.07	4.79	11.89	59.48%	84
	(8.59)	(1.68)	(9.14)		(19.08)	(1.58)	(19.41)		
Norway	4.62	6.72	11.34	40.76%	5.00	4.28	9.22	54.19%	135
	(8.08)	(1.19)	(8.31)		(20.39)	(1.62)	(20.92)		
Portugal	9.29	4.45	13.74	67.60%	8.49	2.54	11.05	76.86%	68
	(10.48)	(1.74)	(11.33)		(36.03)	(1.35)	(36.41)		
Spain	7.20	4.16	11.36	63.38%	6.86	4.65	11.29	60.74%	115
	(12.95)	(1.60)	(13.28)		(19.83)	(2.85)	(20.65)		
Sweden	4.23	7.20	11.43	36.98%	6.95	4.12	11.07	62.81%	130
	(7.52)	(1.54)	(7.90)		(20.11)	(1.03)	(20.71)		
Switzerland	3.85	4.64	8.49	45.31%	5.23	3.35	8.55	61.19%	70
	(6.17)	(0.58)	(6.23)		(19.00)	(1.44)	(19.09)		
UK	5.44	3.94	9.38	58.01%	6.42	4.75	11.25	57.12%	108
	(10.01)	(0.88)	(10.17)		(21.53)	(1.36)	(22.39)		
USA	3.54	5.33	8.87	39.94%	6.70	4.38	11.08	60.45%	125
	(8.24)	(0.75)	(8.40)		(18.22)	(1.57)	(18.45)		

Note: Arithmetic average of annual nominal returns, full sample. Standard deviation in parentheses. Period coverage differs across countries. Consistent coverage within countries.

The higher volatility of equity prices is a persistent feature of all countries and all periods in our sample. Capital gains account for a relatively larger share of equity returns, compared to housing returns, in 11 countries, and a similar share in 5 countries.

Since aggregate equity prices are subject to large and prolonged swings, a representative investor would have to hold on to his equity portfolio for longer in order to ensure a high real return. Aggregate housing returns, on the contrary, are more stable because swings in national house prices are generally less pronounced. National aggregate housing portfolios have had comparable real returns to national aggregate equity portfolios, but with only half the volatility.

6. ACCURACY AND COMPARABILITY OF RISKY RETURNS

This section provides consistency and robustness checks by examining (1) the accuracy of equity returns, (2) the accuracy of housing returns, and (3) the comparability of housing and equity returns.

6.1. Accuracy of equity returns

The literature on returns in equity markets has highlighted two main sources of bias in the data: weighting and sample selection. Weighting biases arise from the fact that the stock portfolio weights for the index do not correspond to those of a representative investor, or a representative agent in the economy. Selection biases arise from the fact that the selection of stocks does not correspond to the portfolio of the representative investor or agent. This second category also includes the issues of survivorship bias and missing data bias arising from stock exchange closures and restrictions. We consider how each of these biases may, or may not affect our equity return estimates in this section. An accompanying Appendix Table A.15 also details the construction of the equity index for each country and time period.

Weighting bias The best practice in weighting equity indices is to use market capitalization of individual stocks. This approach most closely mirrors the composition of a hypothetical representative investor's portfolio. Equally-weighted indices are likely to overweight smaller firms, which tend to carry higher returns and a higher risk. The existing evidence from historical returns on the Brussels and Paris stock exchanges suggests that using equally-weighted indices biases returns up by around 0.5 percentage points, and standard deviation up by 2–3 percentage points (Annaert, Buelens, Cuyvers, De Ceuster, Deloof, and De Schepper, 2011; Le Bris and Hautcoeur, 2010). The size of the bias, however, is likely to vary across across markets and time periods. For example, Grossman (2017) shows that the market-weighted portfolio of UK stocks outperformed its equally-weighted counterpart over the period 1869–1929.

To minimize this bias, we use market-capitalization-weighted indices for the vast majority of our sample (see Appendix Table A.15 and Section L). Where market-capitalization weighting was not available, we have generally used alternative weights such as book capital or transaction volumes, rather than equally-weighted averages. For the few equally-weighted indices that remain in our sample, the overall impact on aggregate return estimates ought to be negligible.

Selection and survivorship bias   Relying on an index whose selection does not mirror the representative investor's portfolio carries two main dangers. First, a small sample may be unrepresentative of overall stock market returns. And second, a sample that is selected ad-hoc, and especially ex-post, is likely to focus on surviving firms, or successful firms, thus overstating investment returns. This second bias extends not only to stock prices but also to dividend payments, as some historical studies only consider dividend-paying firms.[9] The magnitude of survivor bias has generally been found to be around 0.5 to 1 percentage points (Annaert, Buelens, and De Ceuster, 2012; Nielsen and Risager, 2001), but in some time periods and markets it could be larger (see Le Bris and Hautcoeur, 2010, for the case of France).

As a first best, we always strive to use all-share indices that avoid survivor and selection biases. For some countries and time periods where no such indices were previously available, we have constructed new weighted all-share indices from original historical sources (e.g., early historical data for Norway and Spain). Where an all-share index was not available or newly constructed, we have generally relied on "blue-chip" stock market indices. These are based on an ex-ante value-weighted sample of the largest firms on the market, that is updated each year and tends to capture the lion's share of total market capitalization. Because the sample is selected ex-ante, it avoids ex-post selection and survivorship biases. And because historical equity markets have tended to be quite concentrated, "blue-chip" indices have been shown to be a good proxy for all-share returns (see Annaert, Buelens, Cuyvers, De Ceuster, Deloof, and De Schepper, 2011). Finally, we include non-dividend-paying firms in the dividend yield calculation.

Stock market closures and trading restrictions   A more subtle form of the selection bias arises when the stock market is closed and no market price data are available. One way of dealing with stock market closures is to simply exclude them from the baseline return comparisons. But this implicitly assumes that the data are "missing at random"—i.e., that the stock market closures are unrelated to the underlying equity returns. Existing research on rare disasters and equity premiums shows that this is unlikely to be true (Nakamura, Steinsson, Barro, and Ursúa, 2013). Stock markets tend to be closed precisely at times when we would expect returns to be low, such as periods of war and civil unrest. Return estimates that exclude such rare disasters from the data will thus overstate stock returns.

To guard against this bias, we include return estimates for the periods of stock market closure in our sample. Where possible, we rely on alternative data sources, such as listings of other exchanges and over-the-counter transactions, to fill the gap—for example, in the case of World War 1 Germany

---

[9]As highlighted by Brailsford, Handley, and Maheswaran (2012), this was the case with early Australian data, and the index we use scales down the series for dividend-paying firms to proxy the dividends paid by all firms, as suggested by Brailsford, Handley, and Maheswaran (2012).

Table 8: *Returns during periods of stock market closure.*

Episode	Real returns		Nominal returns		Real capitalization	
	Avg.	Cum.	Avg.	Cum.	Avg.	Cum.
Spanish Civil War, 1936–40	-4.01	-15.09	9.03	41.32	-10.22	-35.04
Portuguese Revolution, 1974–77	-54.98	-90.88	-44.23	-82.65	-75.29	-98.49
Germany WW1, 1914–18	-21.67	-62.35	3.49	14.72		
Switzerland WW1, 1914–16	-7.53	-14.50	-0.84	-1.67	-8.54	-16.34
Netherlands WW2, 1944–46	-12.77	-20.39	-5.09	-8.36		

Note: Cumulative and geometric average returns during periods of stock market closure. Estimated by interpolating returns of shares listed both before an after the exchange was closed. The change in market capitalization compares the capitalization of all firms before the market was closed, and once it was opened, and thus includes the effect of any new listings, delistings and bankruptcies that occured during the closure.

(otc index from Ronge, 2002) and World War 2 France (newspaper index from Le Bris and Hautcoeur, 2010). In cases where alternative data are not available, we interpolate the prices of securities listed both before and after the exchange was closed to estimate the return (if no dividend data are available, we also assume no dividends were paid).[10] Even though this only gives us a rough proxy of returns, it is better than excluding these periods, which effectively assumes that the return during stock market closures is the same as that when the stock markets are open. In the end, we only have one instance of stock market closure for which we are unable to estimate returns—that of the Tokyo stock exchange in 1946–1947.

Table 8 shows the estimated stock returns during the periods of stock exchange closure in our sample. The first two columns show average and cumulative real returns, and the third and fourth column—the nominal returns. Aside from the case of World War 1 Germany, returns are calculated by comparing the prices of shares listed both before and after the market closure. Such a calculation may, however, overstate returns because it selects only those companies that "survived" the closure. As an additional check, the last two columns of Table 8 show the inflation-adjusted change in market capitalization of stocks before and after the exchange was closed. This acts as a lower bound for investor returns, because it effectively assumes that all delisted stocks went bankrupt during the market closure.

We can see that, indeed, the hypothetical investor returns during the periods of market closure are substantially below market averages. In line with the reasoning of Nakamura, Steinsson, Barro, and Ursúa (2013), we can label these periods as "rare disasters." The average per-year geometric mean return ranges from a modestly negative –4% p.a. during the Spanish Civil War, to an astonishing –55% p.a. during the Portuguese Carnation Revolution. Accounting for returns of delisted firms is likely to bring these estimates down even further, as evidenced by the virtual

---

[10]For example, the Swiss stock exchange was closed between July 1914 and July 1916. Our data for 1914 capture the December 1913–July 1914 return, for 1915 the July 1914–July 1916 return, and for 1916 the July 1916–December 1916 return. For the Spanish Civil war, we take the prices of securities in end-1936 and end-1940, and apportion the price change in-between equally to years 1937–1939.

disappearance of the Portuguese stock market in the aftermath of the revolution. Having said this, the impact of these rare events on the average cross-country returns (shown in Table 3) is small, around –0.1 percentage points, precisely because protracted stock market closures are very infrequent. The impact on country-level average returns is sizeable for Portugal and Germany (around –1 percentage point), but small for the other countries (–0.1 to –0.4 percentage points).

Lastly, Nakamura, Steinsson, Barro, and Ursúa (2013) also highlight a more subtle bias arising from asset price controls. This generally involves measures by government to directly control transaction prices, as in Germany during 1943–47, or influence the funds invested in the domestic stock market (and hence the prices) via controls on spending and investment, as in France during the Second World War (Le Bris, 2012). These measures are more likely to affect the timing of returns rather than their long-run average level, and should thus have little impact on our headline estimates. For example, Germany experienced negative nominal and real returns despite the WW2 stock price controls, and even though the policies it enacted in occupied France succeeded in generating high nominal stock returns, the real return on French stocks during years 1940–44 was close to zero. Both of these instances were also followed by sharp drops in stock prices when the controls were lifted.[11]

6.2. Accuracy of housing returns

The biases that affect equity returns—weighting and selection—can also apply to returns on housing. There are also other biases that are specific to the housing return estimates. These include the costs of running a housing investment, and the benchmarking of rent-price ratios to construct the historical rental yield series. We discuss each of these in turn in this section. Our focus throughout is mainly on rental yield data, as the accuracy and robustness of the house price series has been extensively discussed in Knoll, Schularick, and Steger (2017) (see also their Online Appendix).

Maintenance costs   Any homeowner incurs costs for maintenance and repairs which lower the rental yield and thus the effective return on housing. We deal with this issue by the choice of the benchmark rent-price ratios. Specifically, the Investment Property Database (IPD) rental yields reflect net income—net of property management costs, ground rent, and other irrecoverable expenditure—as a percentage of the capital employed.[12] The rental yields calculated using the rent-price approach detailed in Section 2.4 are therefore net yields. To enable a like-for-like comparison, our historical benchmark yields are calculated net of estimated running costs and depreciation.

Applying the rent-price approach to net yield benchmarks assumes that running costs remain stable relative to gross rental income over time within each country. To check this, Figure 9 presents

---

[11]The losses in the German case are difficult to ascertain precisely, because the lifting of controls was followed by a re-denomination that imposed a 90% haircut on all shares.

[12]For Australia, we start from the gross yield estimate and subtract running costs and depreciation excluding taxes and utilities, calibrated at 2.2 percent of the house value, following Fox and Tulip (2014) (see in particular Appendix Table A1 in the paper). For Belgium, we construct a gross rent-price ratio using data from Numbeo.com, and scale it down, assuming one-third of gross rent goes towards running costs and depreciation, in line with evidence for other countries.

Figure 9: *Costs of running a housing investment.*

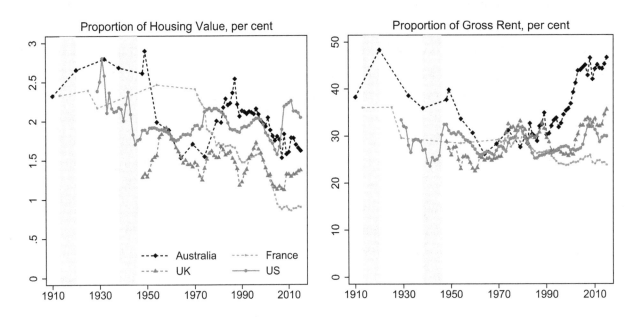

Note: Costs include maintenance, depreciation, and other running expenses such as insurance. Taxes are excluded. Costs are estimated as the household consumption of the relevant intermediate housing input, or fixed housing capital, in proportion to total housing wealth (left panel), or total gross rent (right panel).

historical estimates of running costs and depreciation for Australia, France, UK and USA, calculated as the corresponding housing expenditures and fixed capital consumption in the National Accounts. The left-hand panel presents these as a proportion of total housing value, and the right-hand panel as a proportion of gross rent. We can see that relative to housing value, costs have been stable over the last 40 years, but were somewhat higher in the early-to-mid 20th century. This is to be expected, since these costs are largely related to structure, not land, and structure constituted a greater share of the housing value in the early 20th century (Knoll, Schularick, and Steger, 2017). Additionally, structures themselves may have been of poorer quality. When taken as a proportion of gross rent, however, as shown in the right-hand panel of Figure 9, housing costs have been relatively stable, or at least not higher historically than they are today. This is likely because both gross yields and costs are low today, whereas historically both yields and costs were higher, with the two effects more or less cancelling out. This suggests that the historical rental yields that we have calculated using the rent-price approach are a good proxy for net yields.

Rental yield benchmarking To construct historical rental yield series using the rent-price approach, we start with a benchmark rent-price ratio from the Investment Property Database (IPD), and extend the series back using the historical rent and house price indices (see Section 2.4).[13] This naturally implies that the level of returns is sensitive to the choice of the benchmark ratio. Moreover,

---

[13]For Australia and Belgium, we instead rely on yield estimates from transaction-level data (Fox and Tulip (2014) and Numbeo.com, which are more in line with current-day and alternative historical estimates than IPD.

past errors in rent and house price indices can potentially accumulate over time and may cause one to substantially over- or understate historical rental yields and housing returns.

To check the accuracy of our rental yield estimates, we corroborate them against a wide range of alternative historical sources. These include primary sources in newspapers, as well as economic and financial history books and articles. We also construct additional estimates of rent-price ratios using a procedure related to the *balance-sheet approach* for calculating housing returns. Rather than use directly observed rent-price ratios (in investor portfolios, advertisements, or housing transactions) this approach uses aggregate national accounts data. More precisely, we calculate net rental yield as total rental expenditure less running costs and depreciation, divided by total housing wealth.[14]

Historical sources offer point-in-time estimates which avoid the cumulation of errors, but can nevertheless be imprecise. Primary sources such as advertisements are often tied to a very specific location, and the balance sheet approach relies on a number of approximation and imputation procedures for aggregate data.[15] Because of these uncertainties, we use these alternative approaches to confirm the general level of historical rent-price ratios, rather than their exact value.

In general, these alternative rental yield estimates are close to the values we obtain using the rent-price approach. Figure 10 compares the rent-price approach net rental yield estimates (black diamonds) with those using the balance sheet approach (brown triangles). The first three panels show the time series of the two measures for France, Sweden, and US, and the bottom-right panel shows the correlation between changes in rent-price and balance sheet yields in nine countries (Australia, Denmark, France, Germany, Italy, Japan, Sweden, UK, and US).[16] The level of the rent-price ratio using the two approaches is similar, both in the modern day and historically.[17] The two yield measures also follow a very similar time series pattern, both in the three countries depicted in panels 1–3, and the broader sample of countries summarized in the bottom-right panel.

How representative are the findings of Figure 10? Appendix K provides more detail by comparing our rental yield estimates with alternative approaches for each country. In sum, for most countries and time periods, the rent-price approach and its alternatives match up very well. For some countries and time periods, however, the rent-price yields are somewhat out of line with other estimates. In these cases, we adjust our rental yield series to either benchmark it to historical estimates, or try to correct underlying biases in the rental index that are revealed by this comparison. The largest

---

[14]For reference, the balance-sheet approach to total housing returns estimates one-period gross return on housing H as $H_{t+1} = \frac{HW_{t+1}+REX_t}{HW_t} \times \frac{S_t}{S_{t+1}}$, where HW is housing wealth, REX is total rental expenditure, and S is the value of the housing stock.

[15]For example, rental expenditure of owner-occupiers has to be imputed using census data in benchmark years, housing costs may have to be estimated from higher-level aggregates, and it is difficult to measure housing wealth precisely since it depends on the exact value of all dwellings in the economy, including the underlying land.

[16]We limit our analysis to those countries where balance sheet approach data going back at least several decades were available.

[17]For France, the historical data disagree somewhat, with balance sheet approach estimates both above and below the rent-price approach for some years. We further confirm the housing return series for France using returns on housing investment trusts, documented in the subsequent sections.

Figure 10: *Comparison of the rent-price and balance-sheet approaches for historical rental yields.*

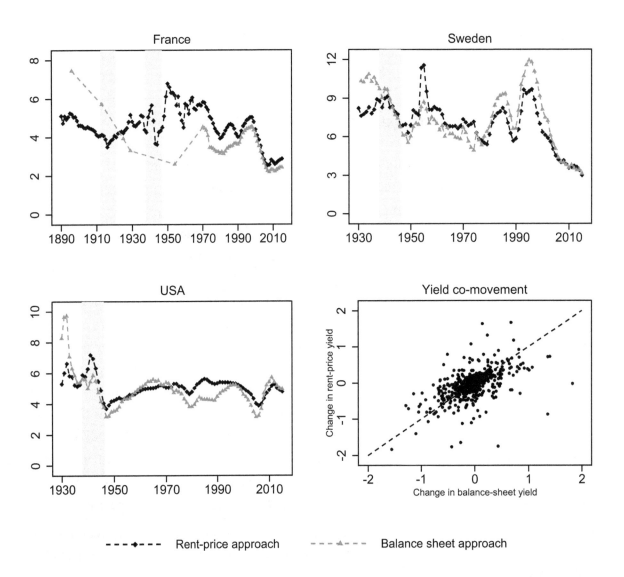

Note: The rent-price approach uses the baseline estimates in this paper. The balance sheet approach estimates the net yield in each year as total rental expenditure less housing running costs and depreciation, in proportion to total housing wealth.

Table 9: *Impact of using different rental yield benchmarks*

	Equity	Housing		
		Baseline	Low benchmark	High benchmark
Mean return p.a.	6.89	7.05	6.26	7.89
Std.dev.	21.94	9.98	9.95	10.09
Geometric mean	4.64	6.61	5.82	7.44
Observations	1739	1739	1739	1739

Note: Average global real returns in 16 countries, equally weighted.

adjustments are made for historical data in Spain and Finland, where statistical agencies seemingly had difficulties computing the rental index during the time of rent controls. Smaller adjustments for more limited time periods are also made for Australia, Denmark, Japan, Norway and Portugal. Each case is explained and detailed in Appendix K. Finally, for two countries, Australia and Belgium, the benchmark IPD yields appear out of line with several alternative estimates for the modern day, leading us to switch to alternative modern-day benchmarks (Fox and Tulip (2014) for Australia and Numbeo.com for Belgium).[18] With these checks and adjustments being in place, we are confident that our rental yields and housing returns are broadly reflective of the historical levels in the respective countries over the past century and a half.

Finally, Table 9 evaluates by how much our housing return estimates are affected by the choice of benchmark yield. For each country, we collect several yield benchmarks: the preferred IPD yield, the balance-sheet approach yield, yields based on rental expenditure and house price data from numbeo.com, and where available, yields computed using detailed transaction-level data (Fox and Tulip, 2014; Giglio, Maggiori, and Stroebel, 2015). We then compute an alternative housing return series using the highest and lowest available benchmark for each country, excluding extreme benchmark yield outliers.[19] For countries where we benchmark to historical rental yields, we use the same historical benchmark for all three series.[20] The first two columns of Table 9 present our baseline real return estimates for equity and housing. The third column shows the average housing return using the lowest benchmark for each country, and the fourth—the average housing return using the highest benchmark. We can see that changing rental yield benchmarks has a small impact on returns, moving them up or down by a little under 1 percentage point. For all benchmark values, returns on housing are similar to those on equity, and housing outperforms equity in compounded (geometric-mean) and risk-adjusted terms.

---

[18]For the US, an alternative benchmark based on the transaction-level data from Trulia is available, as presented in Giglio, Maggiori, and Stroebel (2015). However we do not use it because it is out of line with both the IPD and the balance sheet approach estimates, perhaps because the Trulia yields are not capitalization weighted. For a further discussion, see Appendix K.

[19]The outliers are the numbeo.com yields in Finland, Japan and Sweden.

[20]For example, for Australia, we use a historical benchmark yield in 1949. So the "high" housing return series uses the high rental yield benchmark for 1950–2015, and the historical benchmark for 1900–1949.

Selection, survivorship, and weighting biases To minimise selection bias, we want our house price and rent series to cover a broad geographical area, with the selection and weighting of properties reflective of the portfolio of the representative agent. Knoll, Schularick, and Steger (2017) discuss the selection issues related to the house price series used in this paper. They find that even though some early-period data rely on prices in cities rather than country as a whole, the broad historical house price trends are reflective of countries as a whole, and not just urban centers. For rents, both the IPD benchmark yields, and the historical rental indices have a broad coverage. The selection of properties in the IPD yields, however, may differ somewhat from a representative agent portfolio. On one hand, they are more likely to be concentrated in cities, with the correspondingly lower rental yields. On the other hand, investors may select those properties within a city that have a higher rental yield. The similarity between the IPD yields and whole-country averages computed using the balance sheet approach (see Figure 10 and Appendix K) suggests that these two factors roughly balance out on average.

Next we seek to establish some reasonable bounds of how much the benchmark rent-price ratios are likely to vary with the choice of location. Note that the inverse of the rent-price ratio intuitively can be interpreted as the number of years of annual rent that would be required to purchase the property. In 2013, according to data reported by Numbeo.com, the difference between price-rent ratios in city centers and out of city centers for the countries in the sample in 2013 amounts to a little less than 3 times the annual rent. This motivates us to construct a lower bound rent-price ratio as $RP_{low} = 1/(1/RP_{actual} + 3)$ and an upper bound rent-price ratio as $RP_{high} = 1/(1/RP_{actual} - 3)$ for each country in 2013 to estimate upper and lower bounds of our housing returns depending on the choice of location. Figure 11 shows that this approach results in only a small difference, of about $\pm 1\%$ relative to the baseline estimates.

When it comes to survivorship bias, our price and rental yield estimates aim to capture transaction or appraisal values, and rental costs, on a broad and impartially selected portfolio of properties. Some survivorship bias may, however, enter the series for the following reasons. First, indices that rely on an ex-post selection of cities may inadvertently choose the more "successful" cities over the less successful ones. Second, houses that decline in value are likely to lose liquidity and be sold less frequently, hence carrying a lower weight in the index. And third, chain-linking historical house price and rent indices to compute annual returns will generally ignore the impact of large destructions of the housing stock, in particular those occurring around wartime.

Several factors suggest that the impact of survivorship bias on housing returns should not be too large. First, Figure 11 and Knoll, Schularick, and Steger (2017) show that any location-specific bias in our estimates is likely to be small. Second, if the magnitude of survivorship bias is similar to that in equity markets (Section 6.1), the bias is also unlikely to be large. Third, the low liquidity and weight of houses with declining prices is in some ways similar to the documented negative returns on delisted equities (Shumway, 1997; Shumway and Warther, 1999), which in general cannot be incorporated into the stock return series due to the lack of data. Therefore this bias should be less of a concern when comparing housing and equity returns. Finally, similarly to stock market closures

Figure 11: *Sensitivity of housing returns to the choice of location*

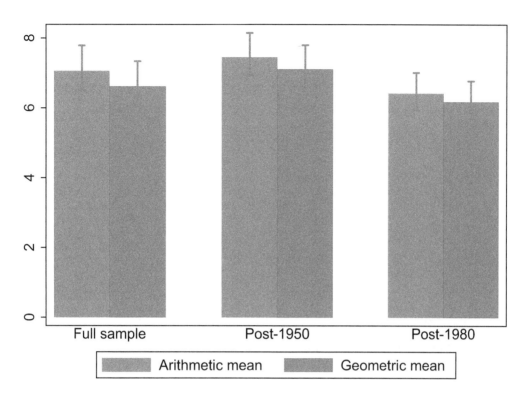

Note: Bars show the arithmetic- and geometric- average housing returns for selected sub-periods. Error bars show the impact of increasing or reducing the benchmark price/rent ratio by ± 3 on historical returns, which broadly captures the difference between in- and out-of-city-center locations.

discussed in Section 6.1, even though capital stock destruction during wars can have a substantial impact on returns in specific years, it is unlikely to profoundly affect cross-country long-run returns due to the rarity of such events.[21] And as Figure 8 shows, the main facts in the data are similar in countries that experienced major war destruction on their own territory and countries that did not (i.e., Australia, Canada, Denmark, and US). Further, Appendix Table A.5 shows that housing offers a similar return relative to equity on average even after wars are excluded.

Returns on real estate investment trusts   Having outlined a number of potential biases, we can further check the plausibility of our housing returns by comparing them to historical returns on housing investment trusts, which offer independent estimates of returns available to a historical representative investor in real estate.

Real estate investment trusts, or REITs, are investment funds that specialize in the purchase and management of residential and commercial real estate. Many of these funds list their shares on the local stock exchange. The return on these shares should be closely related to the performance of the

---

[21] As a reasonable upper bound, existing estimates suggest that around 33–40% of German housing stock was destroyed by Allied bombing during World War 2 (Akbulut-Yuksel, 2014; Diefendorf, 1993), which would lower the country-specific average annual return by around 0.3 percentage points.

Figure 12: *Returns on housing compared to real estate investment funds*

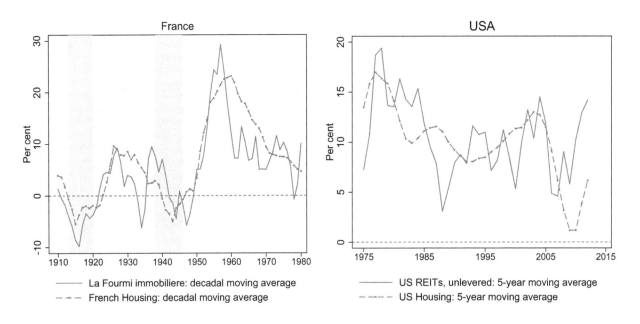

Note: Total real return on housing, and shares of housing investment firms in France and USA. Moving averages. Following Giacomini, Ling, and Naranjo (2015), we assume a 45% leverage ratio for US REITs.

fund's portfolio, i.e., real estate. We would not expect the REIT returns to be exactly the same as those of the representative housing investment. The REIT portfolio may be more geographically concentrated, its assets may contain non-residential property, and share price fluctuations may reflect expectations of future earnings and sentiment, as well as underlying portfolio returns. Further, the REIT portfolio returns should be net of taxes and transaction costs as well as housing running costs, and may therefore be somewhat lower than our housing series. Still, returns on the REIT portfolio should be comparable to housing and can be used to check the general plausibility of our return series.

Figure 12 compares our historical housing returns (dashed line) with those on investments in REITs (solid line) in France and USA, two countries for which longer-run REIT return data are available. For France, the REIT returns series refers to shares of the fund "La Fourmi Immobiliere", whose history is documented by Simonnet, Gallais-Hamonno, and Arbulu (1998). The fund acquired a portfolio of 15 properties in Paris between 1900 and 1913, worth around 36 million euros at 2015 prices, and its shares were listed on the Paris stock exchange between 1904 and 1997. We exclude the period after 1985, when "La Fourmi Immobiliere" was taken over by AGF. For the US, we use the FTSE NAREIT residential total return index after 1994, and the general FTSE equity NAREIT before. To capture the returns on the REIT housing portfolio, REIT returns have to be unlevered. "La Fourmi Immobiliere" had an unlevered balance sheet structure, hence we do not adjust their returns. For the US, we assume a REIT leverage of 45% following Giacomini, Ling, and Naranjo (2015). Returns for France are presented as decadal moving averages, and for the US as five-year moving averages, given the shorter span of the data.

Comparing the solid and dashed lines in Figure 12, the long-run levels of unlevered REIT and housing returns are remarkably similar. The time trend also follows a similar pattern, especially in France. The REIT returns, however, tend to be somewhat more volatile—most likely because they reflect changes in valuation of future earnings, as well as the current portfolio performance. The REIT returns also seem to be affected by the general ups and downs of the stock market: for example, the 1987 "Black Monday" crash and dot-com bust in the US, as well as the 1930s Great Depression and 1960s stock crises in France. This suggests that the valuations of the fund's housing portfolios may be affected by general stock market sentiment.

Overall, the returns on real estate investment funds serve to confirm the general housing return level in our dataset. The comparison also suggests that returns in housing markets tend to be smoother than those in stock markets. The next section examines various factors that can affect the comparability of housing and equity returns more generally.

6.3. Comparability of housing and equity returns

Even if the performance of the fundamentals driving the housing and equity returns (expected dividend/profit, and rental flows) is similar, investor returns on the two asset classes may differ for a number of reasons. These include transaction costs and taxes, as well as differences in the liquidity and financial structure of the investment claim.

Transaction costs The conventional wisdom is that while bonds and equities can be purchased with low transaction costs and at short notice, the seller of a house typically incurs significant costs. We provide a rough estimate of how transaction costs affect our return estimates for housing. To do this, we perform a simple back of the envelope calculation using current data on average holding periods of residential real estate and average transaction costs incurred by the buyer. According to the (OECD, 2012), average round-trip transaction costs across 13 of the 16 countries in our sample amount to about 7.7 percent of the property's value.[22] For the equity market, typical transaction cost values applied to the U.S. are 1.5 bps and 75 bps for the Treasury bill and value-weighted equity returns, respectively. Jones (2002) finds a one-way fee (half-spread) plus commission of 100 bps from the 1930s to the 1970s, implying a round-trip or two-way transaction cost of 200 bps. For less frequently traded stocks, the spreads could be as high or higher, and they could well be higher in overseas markets and in more distant historical epochs.

However, these simple cost ratios need to be adjusted for the typical trading frequency of each asset. According to the American Community Survey of 2007, more than 50 percent of U.S. homeowners had lived in their current home for more than 10 years. Current average holding

---

[22]Data are available for Australia, Belgium, Switzerland, Germany, Denmark, Finland, France, U.K., Japan, the Netherlands, Norway, Sweden, and the U.S. Transaction costs are highest in Belgium amounting to nearly 15 percent of the property value and lowest in Denmark amounting to only 1 percent of the property value.

periods are similar in, e.g., the U.K., Australia and the Netherlands. Accounting for transaction costs would thus lower the average annual return to housing by less than 100 basis points (e.g., 77 basis points per year based on a 7.7% cost incurred every 10 years).

For equities, long-run data gathered by Jones (2002) shows that the turnover, at least post-WW2, has been at a minimum of 25% annually on the NYSE, rising rapidly in recent years. Over a longer horizon NYSE turnover has been at least 50% on average implying annualized round-trip transaction costs of at least 100 bps (e.g., a 200 bps cost on 50% turnover per year) over a century or so. Thus, based on observed average investor holding periods and average investor transaction costs it is clear that the transaction costs on an annualized basis have been not all that different for equities and housing over the long run.

Taxes When calculating equity and housing returns, we do not account for taxes. From an investor's perspective accounting for taxes is clearly important. Equity capital gains and, for some countries and periods, dividend income, are typically subject to a capital gains tax. When dividends are not taxed as capital gains, they tend to be taxed as income. In some countries, housing capital gains are subject to capital gains taxes, but particularly owner-occupied houses have been granted exemptions in many cases. Additionally, housing tends to be subject to further asset-specific levies in the form of property taxes, documented extensively in Appendix M. For both equities and housing, the level and applicability of taxes has varied over time. For housing, this variation in treatment also extends to the assessment rules, valuations, and tax band specifications.

As a ballpark estimate, the impact of property taxes would lower the real estate returns by less than one percentage point per year relative to equity (see Appendix M for further detail). The various exemptions for homeowners make the impact of capital gains taxes on real estate returns even harder to quantify but also imply that differential tax treatment is unlikely to play an important role in explaining the return differentials between equities and housing. Since quantifying the time- and country-varying effect of taxes on returns with precision is beyond the scope of this study, we focus on pre-tax returns throughout the paper.

Temporal aggregation and return averaging Aside from the lower liquidity, the way house price indices and equity price indices are constructed by national statistical agencies is likely to influence the volatility of the return series. House price indices tend to be an *average* of all transactions in a given year, or use a sample of transactions or appraisal values throughout the year. Equity prices, on the contrary, compare *end-of-year* prices of shares. The use of end-of-year rather than yearly-average prices mechanically makes equity returns more volatile.

We can assess the magnitude of this effect by constructing a smooth yearly-average equity return series. To do this, we construct an equity return index based on averages of daily data, and compare it to the same index that instead uses end-of-year values. We do this using daily MSCI equity returns data for 1970–2015. Table 10 presents the end-of-year and yearly-average MSCI real equity returns in the first two columns, and our yearly-average housing returns for the same time period in the

Table 10: *Impact of using end-of-year vs yearly-average asset prices*

	MSCI Equity		RORE Housing
	End-of-year	Yearly average	Yearly average
Mean return p.a.	8.77	7.58	6.57
Std.dev.	27.58	22.04	7.47
Observations	688	688	688

Note: Annual global real returns in 16 countries, equally weighted, 1970–2015. End-of-year returns are computed using the return index value for the last day of the year. Yearly average returns are computed using the average index value throughout the year.

third column. Comparing the first two columns shows that using yearly averages does lower the standard deviation of returns, by around one-fifth, or 5 percentage points. It also lowers the average return by around 1 percentage point, because the return series is a transformation of the raw price data, and lowering the variance of prices reduces the mean of the return. The standard deviation of the smoothed yearly-average equity series is still almost three times that of housing over the same time period.

Because historical house price data sometimes rely on relatively few transactions, they are likely to be somewhat less smooth than averages of daily data. Therefore Table 10 provides an upper bound of the impact of averaging on our return series. Even taking this upper bound at face value, the averaging of house price indices is likely to explain some, but far from all, of the differences in volatility of equity an housing returns.

Spatial aggregation and local versus national diversification In this study, we follow the standard approach and focus on aggregate returns for a representative agent. At the disaggregated level, both individual housing returns and those of individual equities show a higher volatility than the aggregate indices. For example, we found that in the U.S., local (ZIP5) housing return volatility is about twice as large as aggregate volatility, which would about equalize risk-adjusted returns to equity and housing if investors owned one undiversified house. And it is much more difficult to invest in a diversified housing portfolio than a well-diversified equity portfolio.

Having said this, Benhabib and Bisin (2016) show that individual household portfolios in the US mainly consist of risky undiversified private, or unincorporated equity and owner-occupied housing. Our aggregate results suggest that owner-occupied housing offers attractive risk-return characteristics and ample diversification opportunities when compared to individual equity. But to understand exactly how these risk-return characteristics play out at a disaggregated level, a more detailed study of the individual portfolios and the corresponding returns is necessary. This could be a goal of future research.

Leverage The volatility and returns on housing and equity for an individual investor will also be affected by the structure of the investment portfolio, and the way this portfolio is financed. Jordà, Schularick, and Taylor (2016a) show that advanced economies in the second half of the 20th century experienced a boom in mortgage lending and borrowing. It is important to note that this surge in household borrowing did not only reflect rising house prices, but also reflected substantially increased household debt levels relative to asset values. Hence, the majority of households in advanced economies today hold a leveraged portfolio in their local real estate market. As with any leveraged portfolio, this significantly increases both the risk and return associated with the investment. And today, unlike in the early 20th century, houses can be levered much more than equities, in the U.S. and in most other countries. The benchmark rent-price ratios from the IPD used to construct estimates of the return to housing, refer to rent-price ratios of unleveraged real estate. Consequently, the estimates presented so far constitute only un-levered housing returns of a hypothetical long-only investor, which is symmetric to the way we (and the literature) have treated equities.

However, this approach is not truly symmetric for a simple fundamental reason. Computing raw returns to housing and equity indices as above neglects the fact that an equity investment contains embedded leverage since the underlying corporates will have balance sheets with both debt and equity liabilities. Thus, reconciliation is needed, and two routes can be taken. First, for truly comparable raw un-levered returns, the equity returns could be de-levered, to factor out the embedded leverage seen on firm balance sheets. Second, alternatively, for truly comparable levered returns, the housing returns would have to be levered up, to factor in the actual leverage (using mortgages) seen on household balance sheets. Is this a big deal in practice? We argue that it does not bias our conclusions significantly based on some back of the envelope calculations.

Consider, for example, the second reconciliation of levering up housing returns. Let the real long-term safe borrowing rate be r_0, let α be the leverage of the average house proxied by total mortgages divided by the value of the housing stock. Then we can solve for levered real housing returns TR' as a function of un-levered real housing returns TR using the formula $TR' = (TR - \alpha r_0))/(1 - \alpha)$. In our data, representative long-run rounded average values we can use would be $TR = 7.0\%$ and $\alpha = 0.2$, and we can use a long bond return as a proxy for r_0 of around 2.5% p.a. This would imply $TR' = 8.1\%$. In other words, for the representative agent, the levered housing return is about 110 bps higher than the unlevered housing return (8.1% versus 7%), which is a small difference and still leaves equity and housing returns roughly comparable. We conclude that this adjustment is not consequential for the main conclusions we present in this paper. In fact, it would bolster one of our central new claims which is that real housing returns at least match or even exceed real equity returns in the long run when the two are compared on an equal footing.[23]

---

[23]For evidence on α, the average economy wide housing leverage measured by total mortgages divided by the value of the housing stock, see Jordà, Schularick, and Taylor (2016a). If one preferred to use the mortgage rate rather than the long bond in this calculation, the evidence in Zimmermann (2017) points to an average real mortgage rate r_m of around 3% p.a. This would imply $TR' = 8\%$, only slightly lower than the figure quoted in the main text.

7. Risky versus safe returns

Having established the general trends in each risky and safe asset class, we now turn to examine broader patterns of returns across the different asset classes. We start by comparing returns on risky and safe assets. Figure 13 depicts the trends in global safe and risky asset returns, again using decadal moving averages of GDP-weighted global return series. The risky return in each country is a weighted average of housing and equity returns, with weights corresponding to equity market capitalization and housing wealth in each respective country. The safe return is a simple unweighted average of bonds and bills.[24] The left panel of Figure 13 shows the risky and safe asset returns, and the right panel depicts the risk premium, calculated as the risky minus safe difference.

Both risky and safe rates were high during the 19th century but had been gradually declining in the lead to WW1, after which they declined sharply, as is to be expected. After the war, returns recovering during the 1920s. From 1930 onwards, the risky rate has stayed high and relatively stable, whereas the safe rate dropped sharply and remained low until the late 1970s, before increasing and falling back again during the past three decades. These findings have implications for current debates around secular stagnation and the pricing, or mis-pricing, of risk.

Secular stagnation is associated with low rates of return, driven by an excess of savings or a general unwillingness to borrow and invest. These in turn reflect a variety of potential factors, including: (1) lower rates of productivity growth; (2) lower fertility and mortality rates; (3) a decline in the relative price of investment goods; (4) greater firm level market power; and (5) higher income inequality (Eggertsson, Mehrotra, and Robbins, 2017; Rachel and Smith, 2015; Thwaites, 2015).

Indeed, we can see that the safe rate fell sharply during the 1930s, when Hansen (1939) originally proposed the secular stagnation hypothesis. That time also coincided with a demographic bust and was preceded by a big rise in income inequality in the run-up to the Great Depression. The safe rate has been falling again since the mid-1980s as many have noted. Understandably, this has led some observers to suggest that advanced economies are again in danger of entering secular stagnation, e.g., Summers (2014), and Eggertsson and Mehrotra (2014).

But the picture changes radically when we consider the trend in risky returns in addition to safe returns. Unlike safe rates, risky rates have remained high and broadly stable through the best part of the last 100 years, and show little sign of a secular decline. Turning back to the trend in safe asset returns, even though the safe rate has declined recently, much as it did at the start of our sample, it remains close to its historical average. These two observations call into question whether secular stagnation is quite with us. The high and stable risky rate coupled with falling safe rates is also consistent with the notion of a "safety trap" brought about by the shortage of safe assets (Caballero and Farhi, 2017). However with risk risk premiums still not far off their historical averages, the evidence for a safety trap is thus far also not clear-cut.

---

[24]For details on the construction of the weighted returns and the asset weights, see Section 2.3 and Appendix Section E. Appendix Section F further compares the portfolio-weighted returns to equally-weighted returns, i.e., a simple average of housing and equity.

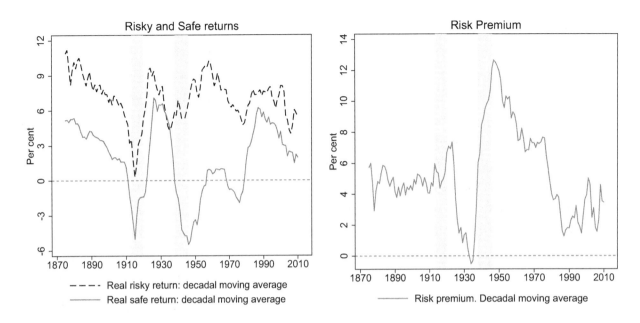

Figure 13: *Global real risky vs. real safe return.*

Note: Mean returns for 16 countries, weighted by real GDP. Decadal moving averages. Within each country, the real risky return is a weighted average of equities and housing, and safe return - of bonds and bills. The within-country weights correspond to the shares of the respective asset in the country's wealth portfolio. Risk premium = risky return - safe return.

We now turn to examine the long-run developments in the risk premium, i.e. the spread between safe and risky returns (right panel of Figure 13). This spread was low and stable at around 5 percentage points before WW1. It rose slightly after the WW1, before falling to an all-time low of near zero by around 1930. The decades following the onset of the WW2 saw a dramatic widening in the risk premium, with the spread reaching its historical high of around 14 percentage points in the 1950s, before falling back to around its historical average.

Interestingly, the period of high risk premiums coincided with a remarkably low frequency of systemic banking crises. In fact, not a single such crisis occurred in our advanced-economy sample between 1946 and 1973. By contrast, banking crises appear to be relatively more frequent when risk premiums are low. This finding speaks to the recent literature on the mispricing of risk around financial crises. Among others, Krishnamurthy and Muir (2017) argue that when risk is underpriced, i.e. risk premiums are excessively low, severe financial crises become more likely. The long-run trends in risk premiums presented here seem to confirm this hypothesis.

Table 11 zooms into the evolution of safe and risky asset returns across different countries and time periods. To enable a comparison with the aggregate trends in Figure 13, we split the post–WW2 period into two subperiods: 1950–1980, when global risk premiums were high and global safe rates low, and post-1980, which saw an initial recovery, and subsequent decline in global safe rates.

The vast majority of the countries in our sample follow similar patterns. The risky rate is largely stable across time, even though it varies somewhat across countries: from just over 5% in Italy and

Table 11: *Real risky and safe asset returns across countries and time*

Country	Full Sample		1950–1980		Post 1980	
	Risky return	Safe return	Risky return	Safe return	Risky return	Safe return
Australia	6.97	1.77	6.51	-1.34	7.74	4.54
Belgium	8.31	1.78	9.68	1.05	7.99	4.27
Denmark	8.15	2.94	8.57	0.49	6.86	4.97
Finland	10.79	2.16	13.47	1.28	12.87	4.18
France	6.69	0.48	12.33	-1.15	7.29	5.15
Germany	7.86	3.34	7.00	1.77	5.18	3.09
Italy	5.28	2.28	7.09	-0.83	5.13	4.14
Japan	6.79	1.29	10.86	0.05	4.81	3.00
Netherlands	7.23	1.31	10.26	-0.89	7.45	3.83
Norway	8.01	1.59	7.75	-2.34	10.53	3.56
Portugal	6.32	0.45	5.19	-3.30	7.15	3.45
Spain	5.30	0.68	7.23	-3.56	5.27	3.96
Sweden	8.51	2.35	8.67	-1.12	11.37	4.05
Switzerland	6.57	1.57	6.01	0.25	7.96	1.84
UK	6.39	1.56	8.31	-1.36	7.73	4.69
USA	6.99	1.85	6.28	-0.44	7.07	3.71
Average, unweighted	7.44	1.88	8.47	-0.82	7.60	3.87
Average, weighted	7.16	1.88	7.80	-0.60	6.54	3.73

Note: Average annual real returns. Real risky return is a weighted average of equity and housing, and safe return - of bonds and bills. The weights correspond to the shares of the respective asset in the country's wealth portfolio. Period coverage differs across countries. Consistent coverage within countries. The average, unweighted and average, weighted figures are respectively the unweighted and real-GDP-weighted arithmetic averages of individual country returns.

Spain to 11% in Finland. Risk premiums were at or near their highest level in almost every country during the period 1950–1980, largely due to low returns on safe assets. The real safe rate of return was close zero or negative for the majority of the countries in the sample, with the lowest level of −3.5% observed in Spain and Portugal, and only Belgium, Finland and Germany experiencing robustly positive real returns. Meanwhile, risky rates were also somewhat above their long-run level in a number of countries, but the differences are relatively smaller than those for safe rates. The post-1980 period saw a recovery in safe rates across the board, with the recent downward trend not yet apparent in these longer-run period averages. Risky rates, meanwhile, were close to their historical levels in most countries, with only Japan experiencing a strong decline following the bursting of its asset price bubble in the 1990s.

We now turn to examine the correlations between risky and safe returns, which are displayed in Figure 14. The top-left panel of this figure shows the rolling decadal correlation between the risky and safe returns, calculated as the average of rolling correlations in individual countries in a similar fashion to the calculations in Figure 7. Throughout most of the historical period under consideration, risky and safe returns had been positively correlated. In other words, safe assets have

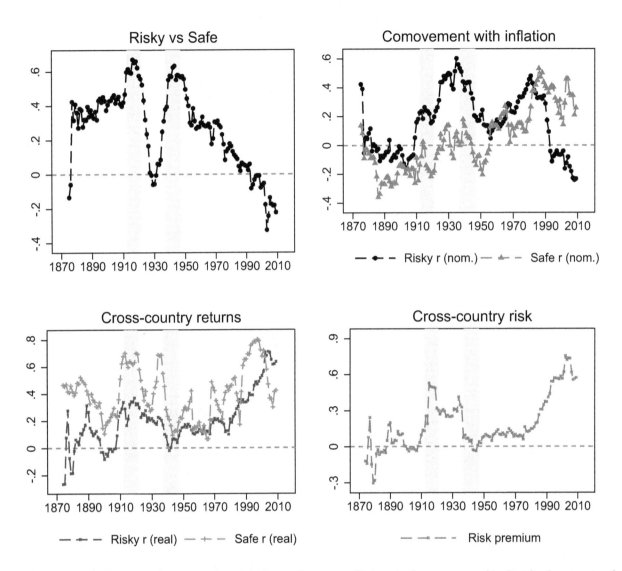

Figure 14: *Correlations across risky asset returns*

Note: Rolling decadal correlations. The global correlation coefficient is the average of individual countries for the rolling window. Cross-country correlation coefficient is the average of all country pairs for a given asset class. Country coverage differs across time periods.

not generally provided a hedge against risk since safe returns were low when risky returns were low—in particular during both world wars—and vice versa. This positive correlation has weakened over the more recent decades, and turned negative from the 1990s onwards. This suggests that safe assets have acted as a better hedge for risk during both the Great Moderation, and the recent Global Financial Crisis.

The top-right panel of Figure 14 shows the comovement of risky and safe nominal returns with inflation. Mirroring the findings presented in the preceding Sections, safe rates have tended to comove more strongly with inflation, particularly during the post-WW2 period. Moving to cross-country correlations depicted in the bottom two panels of Figure 14, historically safe rates in different countries have been more correlated than risky returns. This has reversed over the past decades, however, as cross-country risky returns have become substantially more correlated. This seems to be mainly driven by a remarkable rise in the cross-country correlations in risk premiums, depicted in the bottom-right panel of Figure 14. This increase in global risk comovement may pose new challenges to the risk-bearing capacity of the global financial system, a trend consistent with other macro indicators of risk-sharing (Jordà, Schularick, and Taylor, 2016b).

8. r VERSUS g

Our analysis also provides insights into the debate on inequality. Piketty (2014) and Piketty and Zucman (2014) argue that inequality and wealth-to-income ratios in advanced economies have followed a U-shaped pattern over the past century and a half. They further hypothesize that wealth inequality may continue to rise in the future, along with a predicted decline in the rate of economic growth. The main theoretical argument for this comes about from a simple relation: $r > g$. In their approach, a higher spread between the real rate of return on wealth, denoted r, and the rate of real GDP growth, g, tends to magnify the steady-state level of wealth inequality.

Of course, this is not the only channel through which rates of return can impact the wealth distribution. Rate of return differentials between asset classes can affect the wealth distribution if there are systematic differences in the portfolio composition between rich and poor households as Kuhn, Schularick, and Steins (2017) show, or if rates of returns vary with portfolio size as stressed by Piketty (2014). Studying administrative Swedish data, Bach, Calvet, and Sodini (2016) find that wealthy households earn higher returns on their portfolios, and Fagereng, Guiso, Malacrino, and Pistaferri (2016) use Norwegian tax data to document substantial heterogeneity in wealth returns. Rates of return on wealth are beginning to receive attention in the theoretical literature. For instance, Benhabib and Bisin (2016) point to return differences of assets as one potential channel to explain diverging trends between income and wealth inequality, and Garbinti, Goupille-Lebret, and Piketty (2017) show that price effects played an important role in shaping the French wealth distribution over the past 200 years.

To bring our data to bear on these debates, we construct a measure of the world's real return on wealth as a weighted average of real returns on bonds, equities and housing. We then compare this measure to the rate of real GDP growth of economies over the long-run. Importantly, our approach differs from Piketty (2014) in that we rely on annual returns from observed market prices for each individual asset class, rather than implicit returns derived from aggregate balance sheet data at selected benchmark dates.

Similarly to the risky returns in Section 7, we weigh the individual returns by the size of the respective asset portfolio: stock market capitalization, housing wealth, and public debt (divided equally between bonds and bills).[25] Figure 15 displays the long-run trends in the global real rate of

---

[25]For details on the construction of the weighted returns and the asset weights, see Section 2.3 and Appendix Section E. Appendix Section F further compares the portfolio-weighted returns to equally-weighted returns,

Figure 15: *Real return on wealth and real GDP growth.*

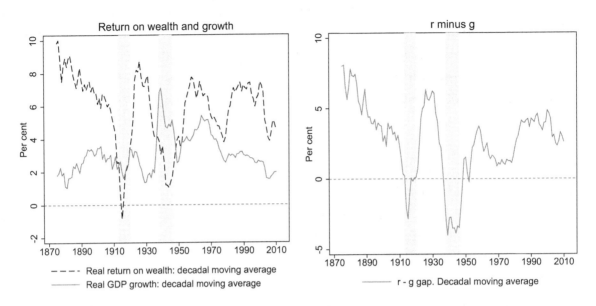

Note: Mean returns and real GDP growth for 16 countries, weighted by real GDP. Decadal moving averages. Within each country, the real return on wealth is a weighted average of bonds, bills, equity and housing. The within-country weights correspond to the shares of the respective asset in each country's wealth portfolio.

return on wealth (dashed line) and the global real GDP growth rate (solid line) since the late 19th century, again using decadal moving averages of GDP-weighted data.

Our data show that the trend long-run real rate of return on wealth has consistently been higher than the real GDP growth rate. Over the past 150 years, the real return on wealth has substantially exceeded real GDP growth in 13 decades, and has only been below GDP growth in the two decades corresponding to the two world wars. That is, in peacetime, r has always exceeded g. The gap between r and g has been persistently large. Since 1870, the weighted average return on wealth (r) has been about 6.0%, compared to a weighted average real GDP growth rate (g) of 3.1%, with the average $r - g$ gap of 2.9 percentage points, which is about the same magnitude as the real GDP growth rate itself. The peacetime gap between r and g has been around 3.6 percentage points.

The real return to wealth has varied over time, with the general long-run level of 6—7 per cent punctuated by four major shocks: the two world wars, with WW2 also including the tail-end of the fallout from the Great Depression; the oil shocks of the 1970s, and the recent Global Financial Crisis. By contrast, real GDP growth rates have remained relatively stable throughout the 20th century, with modest falls during wartime, and a reasonably prolonged elevated level during the post-WW2 reconstruction decades. Consequently, the initial difference between r and g of about 5–6 percentage points disappeared around WW1, and after reappearing briefly in the late 1920s, remained modest until the 1980s. After 1980, returns picked up again while growth slowed, and the gap between r and g widened, only to be moderated somewhat by the Global Financial crisis. The recent decades

with the equally-weighted return on wealth a simple average of equity, housing, and bonds.

Table 12: *Return on wealth and GDP growth across countries and time*

Country	Full Sample		Post 1950		Post 1980	
	Return on wealth	GDP growth	Return on wealth	GDP growth	Return on wealth	GDP growth
Australia	5.91	3.58	7.40	3.85	7.55	3.41
Belgium	6.37	2.31	7.27	2.65	6.87	2.12
Denmark	7.50	2.78	7.24	2.59	6.68	1.76
Finland	9.70	3.58	11.84	3.29	11.66	2.40
France	5.01	2.61	8.24	3.37	6.96	2.07
Germany	6.95	2.84	5.25	2.86	4.70	2.49
Italy	5.05	3.81	5.04	3.29	4.95	1.35
Japan	5.58	4.15	6.33	4.17	4.21	2.04
Netherlands	5.27	3.16	6.68	3.20	6.73	2.28
Norway	6.91	3.06	7.62	3.45	9.25	2.79
Portugal	5.76	3.39	5.53	3.48	6.77	2.12
Spain	4.50	3.21	5.37	4.03	5.18	2.55
Sweden	7.40	2.88	8.66	2.86	9.82	2.35
Switzerland	5.67	2.33	6.06	2.68	7.20	1.94
UK	4.70	2.04	5.92	2.50	7.29	2.45
USA	5.91	3.38	5.77	3.32	6.37	2.80
Average, unweighted	6.28	2.87	6.89	3.25	6.97	2.30
Average, weighted	5.89	3.05	6.01	3.33	5.98	2.48

Note: Average annual real returns. Real return on wealth is a weighted average of bonds, bills, equity and housing. The weights correspond to the shares of the respective asset in each country's wealth portfolio. Period coverage differs across countries. Consistent coverage within countries. The average, unweighted and average, weighted figures are respectively the unweighted and real-GDP-weighted arithmetic averages of individual country returns.

of the widening gap between r and g have also seen increases in wealth inequality (Piketty, 2014; Piketty and Zucman, 2014; Saez and Zucman, 2016).

Table 12 shows how the rate of return on capital and the GDP growth rate have varied across different countries and time periods. Despite some variation, the positive gap between r and g is a persistent feature of the data: r is bigger than g in every country and time period that we consider. The last few decades prior to the Global Financial Crisis saw a general widening of this gap, mirroring the aggregate pattern shown in Figure 15.

As in our previous discussions in this paper, returns on housing play an important part in this story—but with scant data until now, their exact role was less than clear. Rognlie (2015) notes that recent trends in wealth and income could be influenced primarily by what has happened in housing. Real house prices have experienced a dramatic increase in the past 40 years, coinciding with the rapid expansion of mortgage lending (Jordà, Schularick, and Taylor, 2015, 2016a; Knoll, Schularick, and Steger, 2017). This is very much evident from Table 7. Measured as a ratio to GDP, rental income has been growing, as Rognlie (2015) argues. However, the rental yield has declined slightly—given the substantial increase in house prices—so that total returns on housing have remained pretty stable, as we have discussed. Equities display a similar pattern, with post-WW2 increases in total returns coming from capital gains relative to dividends, but with total returns remaining pretty stable. Much of the recent divergence between r and g seems to be coming from a prolonged period of low productivity that started before the Global Financial Crisis (Fernald, Hall, Stock, and Watson, 2017).

Our findings also help shed light on the recent debate about the underlying causes of the declining labor share of income, both in the US (Elsby, Hobijn, and Şahin, 2013) and globally (Karabarbounis and Neiman, 2014) since the 1970s. According to Piketty (2014), the decline in the labor share is simply the flip-side of the rise of capital: with the stock of wealth increasing relative to income, so has the share of factor payments attributed to capital. But this argument hinges on a high elasticity of substitution between capital and labor, such that the extra capital can be put to use without a large decline in its relative price, or the rate of return. Rognlie (2015) has argued that contrary to Piketty's thesis, this elasticity of substitution is low once we account for net, rather than gross income. Recent studies based on US micro-data also estimate a low substitution, including Oberfield and Raval (2014) who use firm-level data, but also account for macroeconomic linkages between firms.

Turning to our data, the first fact that stands out is that there is no clear and stable relationship between $r - g$ and g. The level of $r - g$ was very high during the late 19th century, which was historically a slower growth era in our sample. In the postwar period of fast growth $r - g$ took on a lower average value and remained fairly flat. Over these eras advanced economy growth trends g were subject to a long rise and fall. We find that at an annual frequency correlation of $r - g$ and g is -0.5 in the pre-WW2 and the 1946–1970 peacetime years, but the correlation has fallen to zero in the post-1970 era. Despite the historical negative correlation, the recent experience suggests that falls in g might not substantially drive up the $r - g$ gap. But equally, there is no evidence to suggest that the gap between r and g narrows as the growth rate falls and diminishing returns kick in.

To understand the movements in the labor share, it may therefore be more informative to focus on the return to wealth r itself, and the aggregate stock of wealth, rather than the $r - g$ gap. On that, the macro-historical evidence is somewhat more conclusive. As shown in Figures 15 and 13, the returns to aggregate wealth, and to risky assets have remained relatively stable over recent decades. But the stock of these assets has, on the contrary, increased sharply since the 1970s, as shown in Appendix Figure A.4. The fact that this increase in the stock of wealth has not led to substantially lower returns suggests that the elasticity of substitution between capital and labour may be high, at least when looked at from a long-run macro-historical perspective. The precise reasons for the differences between the macro-historical and micro-driven elasticity estimates, and the mechanisms through which returns on wealth have remained stable while the stock of wealth has increased, all remain fruitful avenues for further research.

9. Conclusion

This paper, perhaps for the first time, investigates the long history of asset returns for all the major categories of an economy's investable wealth portfolio. Our investigation has confirmed many of the broad patterns that have occupied much research in economics and finance. The returns to risky assets, and risk premiums, have been high and stable over the past 150 years, and substantial diversification opportunities exist between risky asset classes, and across countries. Arguably the most surprising result of our study is that long run returns on housing and equity look remarkably similar. Yet while returns are comparable, residential real estate is less volatile on a national level, opening up new and interesting risk premium puzzles.

Our research speaks directly to the relationship between r, the rate of return on wealth, and g, the growth rate of the economy, that figure prominently in the current debate on inequality. A robust finding in this paper is that $r \gg g$: globally, and across most countries, the weighted rate of return on capital was twice as high as the growth rate in the past 150 years.

These and other discoveries set out a rich agenda for future research, by us and by others. Many issues remain to be explored, among them determining the particular fundamentals that drive the returns on each of the asset classes in typical economies. For now, we hope our introduction of this new universe of asset return data can provide the evidentiary basis for new lines of exploration in years to come.

References

Akbulut-Yuksel, Mevlude. 2014. Children of War. The Long-Run Effects of Large-Scale Physical Destruction and Warfare on Children. *Journal of Human Resources* 49(3): 634–662.

Annaert, Jan, Buelens, Frans, Cuyvers, Ludo, De Ceuster, Marc, Deloof, Marc, and De Schepper, Ann. 2011. Are Blue Chip Stock Market Indices Good Proxies for All-Shares Market Indices? The Case of the Brussels Stock Exchange 1833–2005. *Financial History Review* 18(3): 277–308.

Annaert, Jan, Buelens, Frans, and De Ceuster, Marc. 2012. New Belgian Stock Market Returns: 1832–1914. *Explorations in Economic History* 49(2): 189–204.

Bach, Laurent, Calvet, Laurent E., and Sodini, Paolo. 2016. Rich Pickings? Risk, Return, and Skill in the Portfolios of the Wealthy. CEPR Discussion Paper 11734.

Benhabib, Jess, and Bisin, Alberto. 2016. Skewed Wealth Distributions: Theory and Empirics. NBER Working Paper 21924.

Blancheton, Bertrand, Bonin, Hubert, and Le Bris, David. 2014. The French Paradox: A Financial Crisis During the Golden Age of the 1960s. *Business History* 56(3): 391–413.

Brailsford, Tim, Handley, John C., and Maheswaran, Krishnan. 2012. The Historical Equity Risk Premium in Australia: Post-GFC and 128 Years of Data. *Accounting and Finance* 52(1): 237–247.

Caballero, Ricardo J., and Farhi, Emmanuel. 2017. The Safety Trap. *Review of Economic Studies*. Forthcoming.

Campbell, John Y. 2003. Consumption-Based Asset Pricing. In *Handbook of the Economics of Finance*, edited by Constantinides, G.M., Harris, M., and Stulz, R. M., volume 1, chapter 13, pp. 803–887. Cambridge, Mass.: Elsevier.

Cochrane, John H. 2009. *Asset Pricing*. Princeton, N.J.: Princeton University Press.

Cochrane, John H. 2011. Presidential Address: Discount Rates. *Journal of Finance* 66(4): 1047–1108.

Crafts, Nicholas. 2016. Reducing High Public Debt Ratios: Lessons from UK Experience. *Fiscal Studies* 37(2): 201–223.

Diefendorf, Jeffry M. 1993. *In the Wake of War: The Reconstruction of German Cities After World War II*. Oxford: Oxford University Press.

Dimson, Elroy, Marsh, Paul, and Staunton, Mike. 2009. *Triumph of the Optimists: 101 Years of Global Investment Returns*. Princeton, N.J.: Princeton University Press.

Eggertsson, Gauti B., and Mehrotra, Neil R. 2014. A Model of Secular Stagnation. NBER Working Paper 20574.

Eggertsson, Gauti B., Mehrotra, Neil R., and Robbins, Jacob A. 2017. A Model of Secular Stagnation: Theory and Quantitative Evaluation. NBER Working Paper 23093.

Elsby, Michael WL, Hobijn, Bart, and Şahin, Ayşegül. 2013. The Decline of the US Labor Share. *Brookings Papers on Economic Activity* 2013(2): 1–63.

Fagereng, Andreas, Guiso, Luigi, Malacrino, Davide, and Pistaferri, Luigi. 2016. Heterogeneity and Persistence in Returns to Wealth. NBER Working Paper 22822.

Favilukis, Jack, Ludvigson, Sydney C, and Van Nieuwerburgh, Stijn. 2017. The macroeconomic effects of housing wealth, housing finance, and limited risk sharing in general equilibrium. *Journal of Political Economy* 125(1): 140–223.

Fernald, John G., Hall, Robert E., Stock, James H., and Watson, Mark W. 2017. The Disappointing Recovery of Output After 2009. NBER Working Paper 23543.

Fox, Ryan, and Tulip, Peter. 2014. Is Housing Overvalued? RBA Research Discussion Paper 2014-06.

Garbinti, Bertrand, Goupille-Lebret, Jonathan, and Piketty, Thomas. 2017. Accounting for Wealth Inequality Dynamics: Methods, Estimates and Simulations for France (1800–2014). CEPR Discussion Paper 11848.

Giacomini, Emanuela, Ling, David C., and Naranjo, Andy. 2015. Leverage and Returns: A Cross-Country Analysis of Public Real Estate Markets. *Journal of Real Estate Finance and Economics* 51(2): 125–159.

Giglio, Stefano, Maggiori, Matteo, and Stroebel, Johannes. 2015. Very Long-Run Discount Rates. *Quarterly Journal of Economics* 130(1): 1–53.

Goldsmith, Raymond W. 1985. *Comparative National Balance Sheets: A Study of Twenty Countries, 1688–1978*. Chicago: University of Chicago Press.

Grossman, Richard S. 2017. Stocks for the Long Run: New Monthly Indices of British Equities, 1869–1929. CEPR Discussion Paper 12042.

Hansen, Alvin H. 1939. Economic Progress and Declining Population Growth. *American Economic Review* 29(1): 1–15.

Holston, Kathryn, Laubach, Thomas, and Williams, John C. 2017. Measuring the Natural Rate of Interest: International Trends and Determinants. *Journal of International Economics* 108(S1): 59–75.

Homer, Sidney, and Sylla, Richard E. 2005. *A History of Interest Rates.* Hoboken, N.J.: Wiley, 4th edition.

Jones, Charles M. 2002. A Century of Stock Market Liquidity and Trading Costs. Working paper, New York.

Jordà, Òscar, Schularick, Moritz, and Taylor, Alan M. 2015. Betting the House. *Journal of International Economics* 96(S1): 2–18.

Jordà, Òscar, Schularick, Moritz, and Taylor, Alan M. 2016a. The Great Mortgaging: Housing Finance, Crises and Business Cycles. *Economic Policy* 31(85): 107–152.

Jordà, Òscar, Schularick, Moritz, and Taylor, Alan M. 2016b. Macrofinancial History and the New Business Cycle Facts. In *NBER Macroeconomics Annual 2016, Volume 31,* edited by Martin Eichenbaum, Jonathan A. Parker, pp. 213–263. Chicago, Ill.: University of Chicago Press.

Karabarbounis, Loukas, and Neiman, Brent. 2014. The Global Decline of the Labor Share. *Quarterly Journal of Economics* 129(1): 61–103.

Knoll, Katharina. 2016. As Volatile As Houses: House Prices and Fundamentals in Advanced Economies. Unpublished.

Knoll, Katharina, Schularick, Moritz, and Steger, Thomas Michael. 2017. No Price like Home: Global House Prices, 1870–2012. *American Economic Review* 107(2): 331–352.

Krishnamurthy, Arvind, and Muir, Tyler. 2017. How Credit Cycles Across a Financial Crisis. NBER Working Paper 23850.

Kuhn, Moritz, Schularick, Moritz, and Steins, Ulrike I. 2017. Income and Wealth Inequality in America , 1949–2013. CEPR Discussion Paper 20547.

Kuvshinov, Dmitry, and Zimmermann, Kaspar. 2017. Going to the Market. Unpublished.

Le Bris, David. 2012. Wars, Inflation and Stock Market Returns in France, 1870–1945. *Financial History Review* 19(3): 337–361.

Le Bris, David, and Hautcoeur, Pierre-Cyrille. 2010. A Challenge to Triumphant Optimists? A Blue Chips Index for the Paris Stock Exchange, 1854–2007. *Financial History Review* 17(2): 141–183.

Lustig, Hanno, Van Nieuwerburgh, Stijn, and Verdelhan, Adrien. 2013. The Wealth-Consumption Ratio. *Review of Asset Pricing Studies* 3(1): 38–94.

Mehra, Rajnish, and Prescott, Edward C. 1985. The Equity Premium: A Puzzle. *Journal of Monetary Economics* 15(2): 145–161.

Nakamura, Emi, Steinsson, Jón, Barro, Robert, and Ursúa, José. 2013. Crises and Recoveries in an Empirical Model of Consumption Disasters. *American Economic Journal: Macroeconomics* 5(3): 35–74.

Nielsen, Steen, and Risager, Ole. 2001. Stock Returns and Bond Yields in Denmark, 1922–1999. *Scandinavian Economic History Review* 49(1): 63–82.

Oberfield, Ezra, and Raval, Devesh. 2014. Micro Data and Macro Technology. NBER Working Paper 20452.

OECD. 2012. *OECD Economic Surveys: European Union 2012*. Paris: OECD Publishing.

Piketty, T. 2014. *Capital in the Twenty-First Century*. Cambridge, Mass.: Harvard University Press.

Piketty, Thomas, and Zucman, Gabriel. 2014. Capital is Back: Wealth-Income Ratios in Rich Countries 1700–2010. *Quarterly Journal of Economics* 129(3): 1255–1310.

Quinn, Dennis P., and Voth, Hans-Joachim. 2008. A Century of Global Equity Market Correlations. *American Economic Review* 98(2): 535–540.

Rachel, Lukasz, and Smith, Thomas. 2015. Secular Drivers of the Global Real Interest Rate. Bank of England Working Paper 571.

Rognlie, Matthew. 2015. Deciphering the Fall and Rise in the Net Capital Share. *Brookings Papers on Economic Activity* 46(1): 1–69.

Ronge, Ulrich. 2002. *Die Langfristige Rendite Deutscher Standardaktien: Konstruktion eines Historischen Aktienindex ab Ultimo 1870 bis Ultimo 1959*. Frankfurt am Main: Lang.

Saez, Emmanuel, and Zucman, Gabriel. 2016. Wealth Inequality in the United States Since 1913: Evidence from Capitalized Income Tax Data. *Quarterly Journal of Economics* 131(2): 519–578.

Shumway, Tyler. 1997. The Delisting Bias in CRSP Data. *Journal of Finance* 52(1): 327–340.

Shumway, Tyler, and Warther, Vincent A. 1999. The Delisting Bias in CRSP's Nasdaq Data and Its Implications for the Size Effect. *Journal of Finance* 54(6): 2361–2379.

Simonnet, François, Gallais-Hamonno, Georges, and Arbulu, Pedro. 1998. Un Siècle de Placement Immobilier. L'exemple de La Fourmi Immobilière. *Journal de la Société Française de Statistique* 139(2): 95–135.

Summers, Lawrence H. 2014. US Economic Prospects: Secular Stagnation, Hysteresis, and the Zero Lower Bound. *Business Economics* 49(2): 65–73.

Thwaites, Gregory. 2015. Why are Real Interest Rates So Low? Secular Stagnation and the Relative Price of Investment Goods. Bank of England Working Paper 564.

Williams, John C. 2016. Monetary Policy in a Low R-Star World. Federal Reserve Bank of San Francisco Economic Letter 2016-23.

Zimmermann, Kaspar. 2017. Breaking Banks? Bank Profitability and Monetary Policy. Unpublished.

Online Appendix

The Rate of Return on Everything, 1870–2015

A.   The effect of GDP weighting

Figure A.1: *GDP-weighted returns*

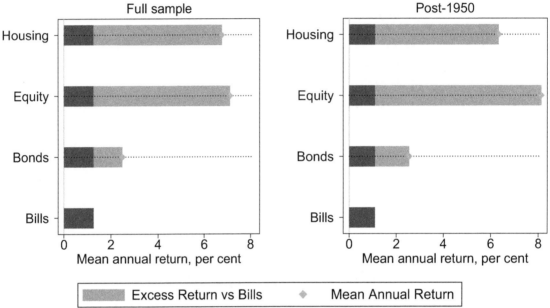

Notes: Arithmetic avg. real returns p.a., weighted by real GDP. Consistent coverage within each country.

This chart shows global average returns for the four asset classes weighted by country GDP, effectively giving greater weight to the largest economies in our sample, namely the U.S., Japan, and Germany. The overall effects are relatively minor. For the full sample, returns on equity and housing are similar at around 7% in real terms. For the post-1950 period, equities outperform housing by about 2pp. on average. The post-1990 housing bust in Japan and the underperformance of the German housing market contribute to this result.

B. More on sample consistency

Throughout the paper, we always use a sample that is consistent within each table and graph, that is, for any table that shows returns on bills, bonds, equity, and housing, each yearly observation has data for all four asset returns. For tables showing bonds versus bills only, each yearly observation has data on both bonds and bills, but may be missing data for equities or housing. At the same time, returns for different countries generally cover different time periods.

Here we investigate whether adjusting for sample consistency affects our results. First, Figure A.2 plots returns for samples that are consistent both within and across countries, starting at benchmark years. The later the benchmark year, the more countries we can include. The resulting return patterns confirm that the basic stylized facts reported earlier continue to hold even under these more stringent sampling restrictions, and regardless of the time period under consideration.

Next, we consider whether going to a fully "inconsistent" sample —that is, taking the longest time period available for each asset, without within-country consistency— would change the results. Table A.1 thus shows returns for the maximum possible sample for each asset. Table A.2, on the contrary, shows returns for a sample that is consistent within each country, across all four asset classes. The results in this table can be compared to Table 3 in the main text. On balance, the choice of the sample makes almost no difference to our headline results.

Figure A.2: *Consistent samples*

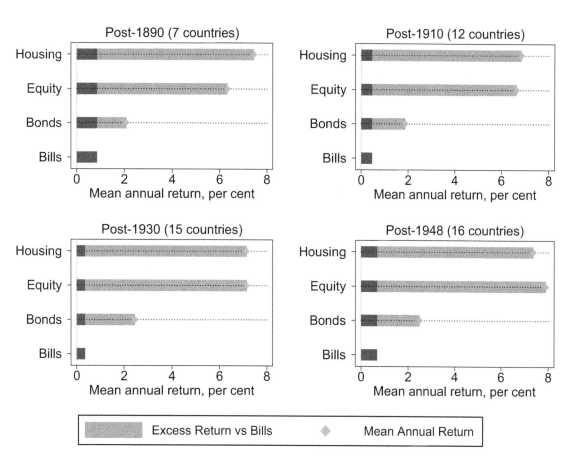

Note: Average real returns p.a. (unweighted). Consistent coverage across and within countries.

Table A.1: *Returns using longest possible sample for each asset*

Country	Bills	Bonds	Equity	Housing
Australia	2.02	2.17	8.41	6.37
Belgium	1.62	3.01	5.89	7.89
Denmark	2.98	3.59	7.22	8.22
Finland	0.64	3.22	9.37	9.58
France	-0.47	0.83	3.25	6.38
Germany	1.49	3.12	8.62	7.82
Italy	1.20	2.11	6.13	4.77
Japan	0.63	2.54	9.69	6.54
Netherlands	1.37	2.71	7.09	7.22
Norway	1.10	2.55	5.95	8.33
Portugal	-0.01	2.76	3.98	6.31
Spain	0.70	1.34	5.41	5.21
Sweden	1.77	3.25	7.96	8.30
Switzerland	1.64	2.41	6.70	5.63
UK	1.16	2.29	7.10	5.36
USA	2.17	2.79	8.34	6.03
Average, unweighted	1.17	2.61	6.99	7.17
Average, weighted	1.32	2.46	7.36	6.66

Note: Average annual real returns. Longest possible sample used for each asset class, i.e. returns are not consistent across assets or within countries. The average, unweighted and average, weighted figures are respectively the unweighted and real-GDP-weighted arithmetic averages of individual country returns.

Table A.2: *Returns using the full within-country-consistent sample*

Country	Bills	Bonds	Equity	Housing
Australia	1.29	2.26	7.75	6.54
Belgium	0.70	2.87	6.78	8.64
Denmark	2.64	3.24	7.20	8.17
Finland	0.08	4.25	9.98	9.58
France	-0.48	1.44	4.06	7.34
Germany	2.65	4.03	6.85	7.82
Italy	1.37	3.19	7.32	4.77
Japan	0.39	2.18	6.09	6.54
Netherlands	0.78	1.85	7.09	7.28
Norway	0.90	2.29	5.95	8.03
Portugal	-0.48	1.37	4.37	6.31
Spain	-0.03	1.39	5.93	5.09
Sweden	1.56	3.14	7.98	8.30
Switzerland	0.81	2.33	6.90	5.77
UK	1.15	1.96	7.20	5.36
USA	1.45	2.26	8.39	6.03
Average, unweighted	1.15	2.62	6.65	7.32
Average, weighted	1.26	2.49	7.11	6.75

Note: Average annual real returns. Returns consistent within countries, i.e. each yearly observation for a country has data on each of the four asset classes. The average, unweighted and average, weighted figures are respectively the unweighted and real-GDP-weighted arithmetic averages of individual country returns.

C. Returns during world wars

Table A.3: *Real returns on risky assets during world wars*

Country	World War 1		World War 2	
	Equity	Housing	Equity	Housing
Australia	0.20	1.22	4.86	4.12
Belgium	-3.75	-5.84	3.12	8.69
Denmark	4.98	4.35	2.85	11.75
Finland	4.68		0.55	-9.79
France	-12.48	-9.37	-4.05	-1.51
Germany	-12.37	-26.53	3.82	
Italy	-6.11			
Japan	15.88			
Netherlands	-0.20	5.07	5.71	9.10
Norway	3.88	-1.38	0.62	2.54
Portugal	-3.99		3.96	
Spain	-5.77	-0.71	-0.73	-4.56
Sweden	-15.72	-3.93	5.56	7.89
Switzerland	-11.19	-4.46	1.32	3.08
UK	-4.04	-0.73	4.56	
USA	0.96	0.06	4.90	8.47
Average, unweighted	-3.03	-1.84	2.65	3.86
Average, weighted	-3.26	-2.02	5.39	6.89

Note: Average annual real returns. We include one year from the immediate aftermath of the war, such that World war 1 covers years 1914—1919, and World War 2 – 1939—1946. Period coverage differs across and within countries. We exclude World War 2 periods for Italy and Japan because of hyperinflation. The average, unweighted and average, weighted figures are respectively the unweighted and real-GDP-weighted arithmetic averages of individual country returns.

The performance of different assets during the major wars is an important issue for asset pricing models that argue that high risk premiums on equities reflect the risk of economy-wide disasters. This argument rests on the work of Barro (2006), developed further in collaboration with Emi Nakamura, John Steinsson and Jose Ursua (Barro and Ursua, 2008; Nakamura, Steinsson, Barro, and Ursúa, 2013). Table A.3 shows the returns of housing and equity markets during World War 1 and World War 2. The data confirm large negative returns in different countries, especially during World War 1. In both wars, housing markets tended to outperform equity, making it potentially more difficult to explain the large housing risk premium that we find. This being said, the positive returns in various countries during World War 2 are in some cases influenced by price controls affecting our CPI measure and direct government interventions into asset markets that aimed at keeping prices up (see Le Bris, 2012, for the case of France). Further, as we do not adjust our return series for changes in the housing stock, the series here underestimate the negative impact of wartime destruction on housing investments. As a result, the war time returns shown here likely mark an upper bound, and wars can still be seen as periods with typically low returns on risky assets.

D.   Returns excluding world wars

Figure A.3: *Returns excluding world wars, full sample*

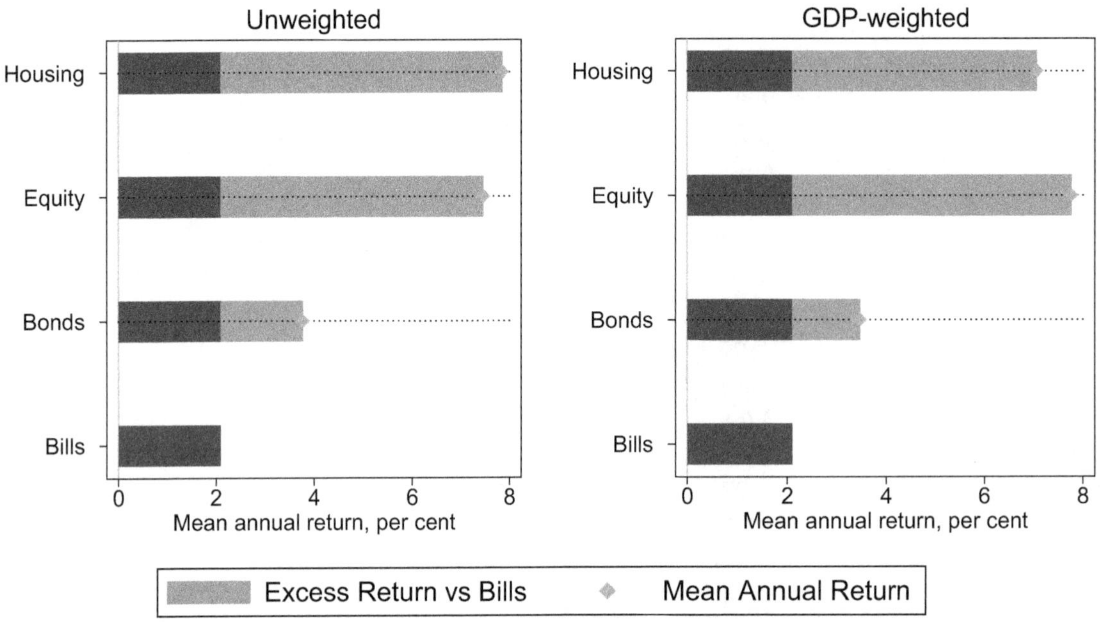

Note: Average real returns p.a., excluding world wars. Consistent coverage within each country.

In Figure A.3 we exclude World War 1 and 2 from the calculation of aggregate returns, but maintain the within country consistency of the sample, as before. As expected, excluding the wars pushes up aggregate returns somewhat, but overall risk premiums and the relative performance of the different assets classes remain comparable.

Table A.4: *Real returns on bonds and bills, including and excluding world wars*

Country	Full Sample		Excluding wars	
	Bills	Bonds	Bills	Bonds
Australia	1.29	2.24	1.73	2.65
Belgium	1.16	3.01	1.77	3.65
Denmark	3.08	3.58	3.80	4.39
Finland	0.64	3.22	2.17	5.34
France	-0.47	1.54	0.89	3.11
Germany	1.51	3.15	2.46	4.06
Italy	1.20	2.53	2.63	4.23
Japan	0.68	2.54	1.85	3.80
Netherlands	1.37	2.71	2.22	3.70
Norway	1.10	2.55	1.91	3.56
Portugal	-0.01	2.23	0.94	3.30
Spain	-0.04	1.41	1.17	2.73
Sweden	1.77	3.25	2.59	4.39
Switzerland	0.89	2.41	1.67	3.47
UK	1.16	2.29	2.03	3.22
USA	2.17	2.79	2.93	3.54
Average, unweighted	1.13	2.61	2.18	3.83
Average, weighted	1.31	2.49	2.24	3.50

Note: Average annual real returns. Returns excluding wars omit periods 1914—1919 and 1939—1947. Period coverage differs across countries. Consistent coverage within countries. The average, unweighted and average, weighted figures are respectively the unweighted and real-GDP-weighted arithmetic averages of individual country returns.

Table A.4 displays country returns for bills and bonds including and excluding war periods. The effect on returns on bonds and bills, both weighted and unweighted, is substantial. The rate of return on bills almost doubles in real terms when the two war windows are excluded, and returns on bonds jump by about 1 percentage point.

Table A.5: *Real returns on equity and housing, including and excluding world wars*

Country	Full Sample		Excluding wars	
	Equity	Housing	Equity	Housing
Australia	7.81	6.37	8.50	6.95
Belgium	6.23	7.89	7.47	8.73
Denmark	7.22	8.10	7.71	7.91
Finland	9.98	9.58	11.66	11.31
France	3.25	6.54	4.87	8.00
Germany	6.85	7.82	7.01	8.13
Italy	7.32	4.77	6.67	4.51
Japan	6.09	6.54	6.85	6.79
Netherlands	7.09	7.28	7.53	7.22
Norway	5.95	8.03	6.39	8.85
Portugal	4.37	6.31	4.37	6.31
Spain	5.46	5.21	6.49	6.41
Sweden	7.98	8.30	9.48	8.97
Switzerland	6.71	5.63	8.25	6.44
UK	7.20	5.36	8.03	5.57
USA	8.39	6.03	9.20	6.14
Average, unweighted	6.60	7.25	7.45	7.87
Average, weighted	7.04	6.69	7.75	7.06

Note: Average annual real returns. Returns excluding wars omit periods 1914—1919 and 1939—1947. Period coverage differs across countries. Consistent coverage within countries. The average, unweighted and average, weighted figures are respectively the unweighted and real-GDP-weighted arithmetic averages of individual country returns.

In Table A.5 we look at the performance of risky assets for the full sample and excluding war periods. The effects are visible, but less strong than in the case of bonds and bills before. Excluding war years pushes up returns on equity and housing by 50 to 80 basis points. These effects are largely independent of the GDP-weighting.

Table A.6: *Real risky and safe asset returns, including and excluding world wars*

Country	Full Sample		Excluding wars	
	Risky return	Safe return	Risky return	Safe return
Australia	6.97	1.77	7.47	2.20
Belgium	8.31	1.78	8.53	2.58
Denmark	8.15	2.94	8.01	3.78
Finland	10.79	2.16	12.60	3.55
France	6.69	0.48	7.60	2.01
Germany	7.86	3.34	8.14	3.36
Italy	5.28	2.28	4.97	2.94
Japan	6.79	1.29	7.11	2.08
Netherlands	7.23	1.31	7.31	2.39
Norway	8.01	1.59	8.81	2.55
Portugal	6.32	0.45	6.32	0.45
Spain	5.30	0.68	6.18	1.96
Sweden	8.51	2.35	9.49	3.41
Switzerland	6.57	1.57	7.43	2.50
UK	6.39	1.56	6.84	2.44
USA	6.99	1.85	7.33	2.65
Average, unweighted	7.44	1.88	8.07	2.93
Average, weighted	7.16	1.88	7.59	2.79

Note: Average annual real returns. Returns excluding wars omit periods 1914—1919 and 1939—1947. Real risky return is a weighted average of equity and housing, and safe return - of bonds and bills. The weights correspond to the shares of the respective asset in the country's wealth portfolio. Period coverage differs across countries. Consistent coverage within countries. The average, unweighted and average, weighted figures are respectively the unweighted and real-GDP-weighted arithmetic averages of individual country returns.

Table A.6 underlines the outperformance of risky assets once we exclude the wars. Average safe returns are about 1 percentage point lower in the full sample, relative to the sample that exclude war years. By contrast, risky returns only rise by between 40 and 60 basis points when we exclude wars. As discussed above the measurement of returns in wars is problematic and we are inclined not to read too much into the relative outperformance of risky assets in war times.

Table A.7: *Return on capital and GDP growth, including and excluding world wars*

Country	Full Sample		Excluding wars	
	Return on wealth	GDP growth	Return on wealth	GDP growth
Australia	5.91	3.58	6.49	3.73
Belgium	6.37	2.31	6.76	2.49
Denmark	7.50	2.78	7.46	2.84
Finland	9.70	3.58	11.57	3.73
France	5.01	2.61	6.19	2.83
Germany	6.95	2.84	7.18	3.00
Italy	5.05	3.81	4.91	3.22
Japan	5.58	4.15	6.29	4.28
Netherlands	5.27	3.16	5.82	3.16
Norway	6.91	3.06	7.69	3.13
Portugal	5.76	3.39	5.76	3.39
Spain	4.50	3.21	5.61	3.44
Sweden	7.40	2.88	8.43	2.96
Switzerland	5.67	2.33	6.62	2.54
UK	4.70	2.04	5.41	2.18
USA	5.91	3.38	6.52	3.18
Average, unweighted	6.28	2.87	7.09	2.94
Average, weighted	5.89	3.05	6.59	2.97

Note: Average annual real returns. Returns excluding wars omit periods 1914—1919 and 1939—1947. Real return on wealth is a weighted average of bonds, bills, equity and housing. The weights correspond to the shares of the respective asset in each country's wealth portfolio. Period coverage differs across countries. Consistent coverage within countries. The average, unweighted and average, weighted figures are respectively the unweighted and real-GDP-weighted arithmetic averages of individual country returns.

Table A.7 looks at the effects of war periods on the aggregate return on capital and GDP growth on a country level and for the global sample. The aggregate return on capital is about 75 basis points higher outside world wars, while GDP growth rates are barely affected as the war effort boosted GDP in many countries in the short term.

E. The global asset portfolio

Figure A.4: *Assets considered in this study as a share of GDP*

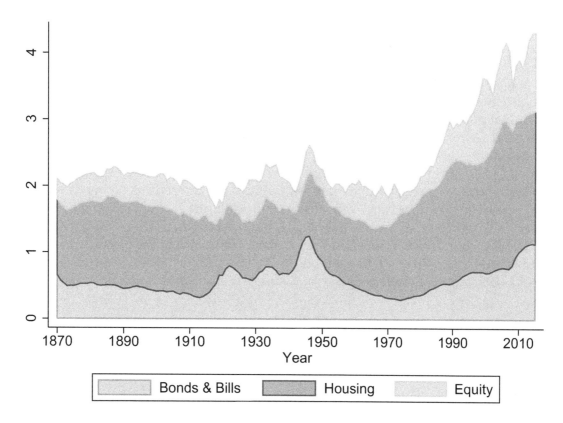

Note: Average of asset-to-GDP shares in individual countries, weighted by real GDP. Equity is the total stock market capitalization. Housing is the stock of housing wealth. Bonds and bills are the stock of public debt.

This section briefly presents the asset portfolio data used to calculate the weighted risky and safe asset returns, and the overall rate of return on capital. As outlined in Section 2.3, we weight the individual asset returns within each country according to the market-capitalization shares of the respective asset types in the country's investible wealth portfolio, to arrive at these composite return measures. (Thus, by this choice of method, significant non-market asset weights are not included, notably non-traded equity wealth.)

We measure equity wealth as the stock market capitalization of the specific country, using the newly collected data from Kuvshinov and Zimmermann (2017). These data strive to measure the total size of the domestic stock market, excluding foreign-owned companies, and aggregating across multiple stock exchanges within the country, excluding cross listings, at each year in the historical sample. Due to data limitations we have had to rely on data for individual markets for a number of countries and historical periods (e.g., only counting the Lisbon listings, but not the Porto listings for Portugal), and rely on interpolation to construct some of the early annual estimates. The stock market capitalization data are sourced from a wide variety of publications in academic journals, historical statistical publications, and disaggregated data on stock listings and company reports of listed firms.

To measure the value of housing wealth for each country, we went back to the historical national wealth data to trace the value of buildings and the underlying land over the past 150 years.

We heavily relied on the national wealth estimates by Goldsmith (Garland and Goldsmith, 1959; Goldsmith, 1962, 1985) as well as the on the collection of national wealth estimates from Piketty and Zucman (2014) for the pre-WW2 period. We also drew upon the work of economic and financial historians, using the national wealth estimates of Stapledon (2007) for Australia, Abildgren (2016) for Denmark, Artola Blanco, Bauluz, and Martínez-Toledano (2017) for Spain, Waldenström (2017) for Sweden, and Saez and Zucman (2016) for the US. For the postwar decades, we turned to published and unpublished data from national statistical offices such as the U.K. Office of National Statistics or Statistics Netherlands (1959). Particularly for the earlier periods, many of the sources provided estimates for benchmark years rather than consistent time series of housing wealth. In these cases, we had to use interpolation to arrive at annual estimates.

We use total public debt from the latest vintage of the long-run macrohistory database (Jordà, Schularick, and Taylor, 2016) as a proxy for the stock of bonds and bills, and divide public debt equally between these two financial instruments.

The broad patterns in the asset holdings show that housing has been the dominant asset in the countries' portfolios throughout the sample. Public debt, and returns on bonds and bills, have tended to increase in size after wars, and most recently after the Global Financial Crisis. The stock market has tended to be small relative to housing, but has increased in size during the last several decades. The last four decades have also seen a marked increase in the aggregate stock of assets pictured in Figure A.4, in line with the findings of Piketty and Zucman (2014), who cover a broader selection of assets, but have fewer countries and observations in their sample.

F. Equally-weighted portfolio returns

Table A.8: *Equally-weighted portfolio returns*

Country	Portfolio weights		Equal weights	
	Risky return	Return on wealth	Risky return	Return on wealth
Australia	6.97	5.91	7.14	5.51
Belgium	8.31	6.37	7.71	6.10
Denmark	8.15	7.50	7.69	6.21
Finland	10.79	9.70	9.78	7.94
France	6.69	5.01	5.70	4.28
Germany	7.86	6.95	7.33	6.23
Italy	5.28	5.05	6.04	5.09
Japan	6.79	5.58	6.31	4.94
Netherlands	7.23	5.27	7.18	5.40
Norway	8.01	6.91	6.99	5.42
Portugal	6.32	5.76	5.34	4.02
Spain	5.30	4.50	5.51	4.14
Sweden	8.51	7.40	8.14	6.48
Switzerland	6.57	5.67	6.33	5.00
UK	6.39	4.70	6.28	4.84
USA	6.99	5.91	7.21	5.56
Average, unweighted	7.44	6.28	6.99	5.53
Average, weighted	7.16	5.89	6.93	5.45

Note: Average annual real returns for the full sample. The portfolio-weighted averages use country-specific stocks of housing, equity, bonds and bills as weights for the individual asset returns. Portfolio-weighted risky return is a weighted average of housing and equity, using stock market capitalization and hosuing wealth as weights. Portfolio-weighted real return on wealth is a weighted average of equity, housing, bonds and bills, using stock market capitalization, housing wealth and public debt stock as weights. Equally-weighted risky return is an unweighted average of housing an equity. Equally-weighted return on wealth is an unweighted average of housing, equity and bonds. Period coverage differs across countries. Consistent coverage within countries. The average, unweighted and average, weighted figures are respectively the unweighted and real-GDP-weighted arithmetic averages of individual country returns.

Table A.8 assesses the impact of portfolio weighting on our return estimates. The weighting has a relatively small impact on the risky rates, because returns on housing and equity are generally similar. It raises the return on capital by around one percentage point, because the outstanding stock of public debt is substantially smaller than that of risky assets. The basic stylized facts of $r \gg g$, and high long-run risky returns continue to hold regardless of the weighting, both on average and across the individual countries in our sample.

G. US Dollar returns

Table A.9: *Global real returns for a US-Dollar investor*

	Real returns				Nominal Returns			
	Bills	Bonds	Equity	Housing	Bills	Bonds	Equity	Housing
Full sample:								
Mean return p.a.	1.87	3.44	7.84	8.11	4.44	5.98	10.54	10.91
Std.dev.	12.12	15.60	25.08	15.83	11.70	14.91	25.35	16.19
Geometric mean	1.08	2.23	4.94	6.91	3.71	4.90	7.68	9.70
Mean excess return p.a.	0.23	1.80	6.20	6.47				
Std.dev.	11.30	14.71	24.72	15.82				
Geometric mean	-0.46	0.73	3.37	5.28				
Observations	1739	1739	1739	1739	1739	1739	1739	1739
Post-1950:								
Mean return p.a.	2.13	3.99	9.45	8.91	5.74	7.61	13.20	12.75
Std.dev.	10.59	13.78	26.15	14.92	10.97	13.90	26.67	15.36
Geometric mean	1.59	3.10	6.36	7.93	5.18	6.74	10.13	11.74
Mean excess return p.a.	0.80	2.66	8.12	7.58				
Std.dev.	10.58	13.82	25.91	15.03				
Geometric mean	0.25	1.74	5.05	6.56				
Observations	1016	1016	1016	1016	1016	1016	1016	1016

Note: Global average US-Dollar returns, equally weighted. Real returns subtract US inflation. Excess returns are over US Treasury bills. Period coverage differs across countries. Consistent coverage within countries.

Table A.9 shows nominal and real returns from the perspective of a US-Dollar investor. The Table can be directly compared to Table 3 in the paper. Overall, calculating returns in dollars increases their volatility, since returns now also fluctuate with nominal exchange rate movements. It also adds up to 1 percentage point to the local currency returns reported in Table 3. The higher average return is, for the most part, driven by the higher volatility—exchange rate movements amplify both positive and negative returns, but because returns are on average positive, the average return increases. The effects are stronger after World War 2, going hand-in-hand with the greater exchange rate volatility after the collapse of the Bretton Woods system.

Table A.10: *USD returns by country*

Country	Bills	Bonds	Equity	Housing
Australia	1.69	2.51	8.48	7.20
Belgium	0.81	3.19	7.29	8.83
Denmark	3.41	4.00	7.87	8.94
Finland	1.83	6.39	11.93	11.90
France	1.05	3.04	5.21	9.10
Germany	4.25	5.74	8.41	9.61
Italy	2.74	4.70	8.64	6.26
Japan	2.25	4.03	7.84	8.61
Netherlands	1.79	2.86	7.94	8.60
Norway	1.58	2.98	7.05	8.81
Portugal	0.10	1.98	5.71	6.96
Spain	0.85	2.28	6.87	6.30
Sweden	2.02	3.58	8.56	8.81
Switzerland	1.97	3.55	7.74	7.06
UK	1.87	2.72	8.02	6.15
USA	1.45	2.26	8.39	6.03
Average, unweighted	2.00	3.53	7.60	8.33
Average, weighted	1.98	3.25	7.84	7.57

Note: Average annual real US-Dollar returns. Calculated as nominal US-Dollar return minus US inflation. Period coverage differs across countries. Consistent coverage within countries. The average, unweighted and average, weighted figures are respectively the unweighted and real-GDP-weighted arithmetic averages of individual country returns.

In Table A.10 we display Dollar returns for individual asset classes and individual countries for the full sample. For US-Dollar based fixed income investors, Germany and Finland offered the highest returns. In housing markets, Germany and Finland again stand out, and high returns are seen in Belgium, France, Netherlands and the Scandinavian countries. In equity markets, Finland, Italy and Sweden were the best performing markets.

H. Risky returns ranked by country

Table A.11: *Risky returns ranked by country*

Country	Full sample	Post-1950	Post-1980
Finland	10.79	12.99	12.87
Sweden	8.51	10.21	11.37
Belgium	7.60	8.72	7.99
Denmark	8.09	7.86	6.86
Norway	8.01	9.26	10.53
Germany	7.86	5.81	5.18
Average, unweighted	7.44	8.07	7.60
Netherlands	7.23	8.79	7.45
USA	6.99	6.88	7.07
Australia	6.97	8.45	7.74
Japan	6.79	7.04	4.81
France	6.69	9.68	7.29
Switzerland	6.57	7.13	7.96
UK	6.39	7.88	7.73
Portugal	6.32	6.06	7.15
Spain	5.30	6.03	5.27
Italy	5.28	5.80	5.13

Note: Average annual real risky returns. Real risky return is a weighted average of equity and housing. The weights correspond to the shares of the respective asset in the country's wealth portfolio. Period coverage differs across countries. Consistent coverage within countries. The figure is the unweighted arithmetic average of individual country returns.

In Table A.11 we rank risky returns in the different countries. We calculate risky returns as a combination of equity and housing weighted by the share of each asset in the country's total wealth portfolio. North-western Europe—essentially the Scandinavian countries plus Germany and Belgium—stands out as the region with the highest aggregate returns on risky assets. The U.S. returns are about average, while the southern European countries have comparatively low long-run returns.

I. Returns before the Global Financial Crisis

Table A.12: *Asset returns before the Global Financial Crisis*

Country	Bills	Bonds	Equity	Housing
Australia	1.30	1.95	8.28	6.49
Belgium	1.32	2.86	6.07	8.22
Denmark	3.31	3.56	6.81	8.67
Finland	0.76	3.10	10.64	9.96
France	-0.46	1.17	3.14	6.68
Germany	1.64	3.13	6.94	7.80
Italy	1.30	2.24	8.26	5.32
Japan	0.74	2.51	6.20	6.88
Netherlands	1.48	2.50	7.11	7.77
Norway	1.14	2.41	6.15	8.14
Portugal	-0.00	1.64	5.71	7.19
Spain	0.01	0.95	5.84	5.89
Sweden	1.86	3.09	7.87	8.32
Switzerland	0.99	2.17	6.81	5.40
UK	1.32	2.16	7.52	5.67
USA	2.36	2.65	8.47	6.22
Average, unweighted	1.23	2.42	6.73	7.49
Average, weighted	1.43	2.34	7.14	6.90

Note: Average annual real returns excluding the Global Financial Crisis (i.e. sample ends in 2007). Period coverage differs across countries. Consistent coverage within countries. The average, unweighted and average, weighted figures are respectively the unweighted and real-GDP-weighted arithmetic averages of individual country returns.

This Table cuts the sample off in 2007, i.e., before the Global Financial Crisis. Comparing this table to Tables 4 and 5 in the main text shows that the effects are relatively minor. The crisis only shaves off about 10-20 basis points from equity and housing returns, and adds about 10 basis points to bills and bonds.

Table A.13: *Risky and safe returns, including and exluding the GFC*

Country	Full Sample		Excluding the GFC	
	Risky return	Safe return	Risky return	Safe return
Australia	6.97	1.77	7.18	1.63
Belgium	8.31	1.78	8.58	1.77
Denmark	8.15	2.94	8.39	3.04
Finland	10.79	2.16	11.36	2.19
France	6.69	0.48	6.80	0.39
Germany	7.86	3.34	7.86	3.49
Italy	5.28	2.28	5.89	2.18
Japan	6.79	1.29	7.01	1.28
Netherlands	7.23	1.31	7.58	1.19
Norway	8.01	1.59	8.15	1.52
Portugal	6.32	0.45	7.24	-0.26
Spain	5.30	0.68	5.97	0.47
Sweden	8.51	2.35	8.46	2.30
Switzerland	6.57	1.57	6.50	1.49
UK	6.39	1.56	6.72	1.57
USA	6.99	1.85	7.09	1.84
Average, unweighted	7.44	1.88	7.65	1.84
Average, weighted	7.16	1.88	7.32	1.86

Note: Average annual real returns excluding the Global Financial Crisis (i.e. sample ends in 2007). Real risky return is a weighted average of equity and housing, and safe return - of bonds and bills. The weights correspond to the shares of the respective asset in the country's wealth portfolio. Period coverage differs across countries. Consistent coverage within countries. The average, unweighted and average, weighted figures are respectively the unweighted and real-GDP-weighted arithmetic averages of individual country returns.

This Table recalculates risky and safe returns including and excluding the Global Financial Crisis on a country level and for the global average. As noted before, the effects are quantitatively small. Excluding the crisis boosts risky returns by 10-20 basis, and lower safe returns by no more than 5 basis points. In light of the long time horizon of nearly 150 years, asset performance in the recent crisis plays a minor role for the returns presented here.

J. Data overview

Table A.14: *Overview of bill and bond data*

Country	Bills		Bonds	
	Period	Type of rate	Period	Type of bond
Australia	1870–1928	Deposit rate	1900–1968	Long maturity, central gov't
	1929–1944	Money market rate	1969–2015	Approx. 10y, central gov't
	1948–2015	Government bill rate		
Belgium	1870–1899	Central bank discount rate	1870–1913	Perpetual
	1900–1964	Deposit rate	1914–1940	Long maturity, central gov't
	1965–2015	Government bill rate	1941–1953	Perpetual
			1954–2015	Approx. 10y, central gov't
Denmark	1875–2015	Money market rate	1870–1923	Perpetual
			1924–1979	Long maturity, central gov't
			1980–2015	Approx. 10y, central gov't
Finland	1870–1977	Money market rate	1870–1925	Long maturity, central gov't
	1978–2015	Interbank rate	1926–1991	Approx. 5y, central gov't
			1992–2015	Approx. 10y, central gov't
France	1870–1998	Money market rate	1870–1969	Perpetual
	1999–2015	Government bill rate	1970–2015	Long maturity, central gov't
Germany	1870–1922	Money market rate	1870–1878	Long maturity, local gov't
	1924–1944	Interbank rate	1879–1943	Long maturity, central gov't
	1950–2015	Money market rate	1948–1955	Mortgage bond
			1956–2015	Long maturity, central gov't
Italy	1870–1977	Money market rate	1870–1913	Perpetual
	1978–2015	Government bill rate	1914–1954	Long maturity, central gov't
			1955–2015	Approx. 10y, central gov't
Japan	1876–1956	Deposit rate	1881–1970	Long maturity, central gov't
	1957–2015	Money market rate	1971–2015	Approx. 10y, central government
Netherlands	1870–1957	Money market rate	1870–1899	Perpetual
	1958–1964	Central bank discount rate	1900–1987	Long maturity, central gov't
	1965–2015	Money market rate	1988–2015	Approx. 10y, central government
Norway	1870–2015	Deposit rate	1870–1919	Long maturity, central gov't
			1920–2015	Approx. 10y, central gov't
Portugal	1880–1914	Money market rate	1870–1974	Long maturity, central gov't
	1915–1946	Central bank discount rate	1975–2015	Approx. 10y, central gov't
	1947–1977	Deposit rate		
	1978–2015	Money market rate		
Spain	1870–1921	Money market rate	1900–1990	Long maturity, central gov't
	1922–1974	Deposit rate	1991–2015	Approx. 10y, central government
	1975–2015	Money market rate		
Sweden	1870–1998	Deposit rate	1874–1918	Long maturity, central gov't
	1999–2015	Government bill rate	1919–1949	Perpetual
			1950–2015	Approx. 10y, central gov't
Switzerland	1870–1968	Deposit rate	1900–1984	Long maturity, central gov't
	1969–2015	Money market rate	1985–2015	Approx. 10y, central gov't
United Kingdom	1870–2015	Money market rate	1870–1901	Perpetual
			1902–1979	Long maturity, central gov't
			1980–2015	Approx. 10y, central gov't
United States	1870–2013	Deposit rate	1870–1926	Approx. 10y, central gov't
	2014–2015	Money market rate	1927–2015	Long maturity, central gov't

Table A.15: *Overview of equity and housing data*

Country	Equity			Housing	
	Period	Coverage	Weighting	Period	Coverage
Australia	1870–1881	Listed abroad	Market cap	1901–2015	Urban
	1882–2015	Broad	Market cap		
Belgium	1870–2015	All share	Market cap	1890–1950	Urban
				1951–1961	Mixed
				1977–2015	Nationwide
Denmark	1893–1914	Broad	Book cap	1876–1964	Mixed
	1915–1999	Broad	Market cap	1965–2015	Nationwide
	2000–2015	Blue chip	Market cap	1965–2015	Nationwide
Finland	1896–1911	Broad	Book cap	1920–1964	Urban
	1912–1969	All share	Market cap	1965–1969	Mixed
	1970–1990	Broad	Market cap	1970–2015	Nationwide
	1991–2015	All share	Market cap		
France	1870–2015	Blue chip	Market cap	1871–1935	Urban
				1936–1948	Mixed
				1949–2015	Nationwide
Germany	1870–1913	All share	Market cap	1871–1912	Mixed
	1914–1959	Blue chip	Market cap	1913–1938	Urban
	1960–2015	Broad	Market cap	1939–1947	Mixed
				1948–1970	Nationwide
				1971–2015	Mixed
Italy	1870–1887	Selected stocks	Book cap	1928–1998	Urban
	1888–2015	Broad	Market cap	1999–2015	Mixed
Japan	1882–1975	Broad	Transaction volume	1931–1946	Urban
	1976–2004	All share	Mix of equal and market cap	1947–2015	Mixed
	2005–2015	Broad	Market cap		
Netherlands	1900–2015	Broad	Mostly market cap	1871–1969	Mixed
Norway	1881–1914	All share	Market cap	1871–2015	Urban
	1915–1955	All share	Mix of equal and book cap		
	1956–2000	All share	Mix of book cap and company turnover		
	2001–2015	Blue chip	Market cap		
Portugal	1871–1987	All share	Market cap	1948–2015	Mixed
	1988–2015	Blue chip	Market cap		
Spain	1900–1969	All share	Market cap	1901–1957	Mixed
	1970–1987	Blue chip	Market cap	1958–2015	Nationwide
	1988–2015	All share	Market cap		
Sweden	1871–2015	Broad	Market cap	1883-1959	Urban
				1960–2015	Mixed
Switzerland	1900–1925	All share	Market cap	1902–1930	Urban
	1926–1959	Broad	Equally weighted	1931–1940	Mixed
	1960–2015	Broad	Market cap	1941–2015	Nationwide
United Kingdom	1870–1928	All share	Market cap	1900–1913	Mixed
	1929–1963	Blue chip	Market cap	1914–1929	Urban
	1964–2015	All share	Market cap	1930–1946	Mixed
				1947–2015	Nationwide
United States	1872–2015	Broad	Market cap	1891–1952	Urban
				1953–2015	Mixed

K.   Housing returns

This section details construction of the rental yield series for each country. For details on the house price data, please see Knoll, Schularick, and Steger (2017).

As described in Section 2.3, the baseline housing return series is constructed using the rent-price approach. To do this, we take a benchmark net rent-price ratio—adjusted down for maintenance and other costs—in the year 2012, 2013 or 2014, and extrapolate it back using growth in the house price and rent indices. For this purpose, we use the house price index presented by Knoll, Schularick, and Steger (2017) and the rent index introduced in Knoll (2016). We further check the rent-price approach estimates against various alternative historical benchmarks. These include the balance sheet approach constructed from National Accounts data (see Section 6.2 for more detail on this method), and independent estimates from books, journal articles and historical newspapers.

If the rent-price approach estimate differs substantially from those in the alternative sources, we adjust it so that the estimates are in line with each other. We do not adjust the series when these differences are small, or we have good reasons to doubt the quality of the alternative estimates. When we do adjust, we either benchmark our series to historical net rent-price ratios from alternative sources, or adjust the growth in the rental index by a multiplicative factor, such that the different estimates of historical rent-price ratios are broadly in line with each other.

In each of the Appendix Figures A.5—A.20, the series that we use in the paper are the "Rent-price ratio, final series" estimates denoted as green circles. These incorporate any adjustments made to bring the data into line with historical sources. Alongside these, we also present the raw unadjusted rent-price approach series—orange circles—and the alternative historical estimates themselves. We also show alternative benchmark estimates for the present day to help assess the reliability of our baseline IPD rent-price ratio. These are generally sourced from data on rental expenditure and property values on Numbeo.com, for one- and three-bedroom apartments i). within city-centres and ii). in the rest of the country, and are adjusted down by us to proxy the impact of running costs and depreciation. For cases where data on running costs and depreciation were not available, we estimate these to be about one-third of gross rent, in line with the recent and historical experience in most countries (see Figure 9). For Australia and USA, we additionally make use of benchmark rent-price ratio estimates based on detailed transaction-level data. In two countries—Australia and Belgium—we judge one of these alternative modern-day benchmarks to be more reliable than the IPD ratio, and use it to construct our final baseline net rent-price ratio series.

Australia

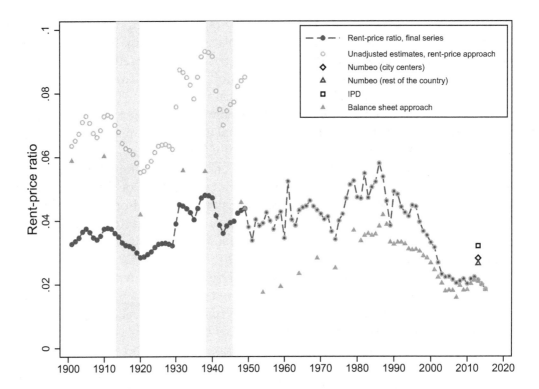

For 2014, Fox and Tulip (2014) report a gross rental yield of 4.2 per cent, running costs excluding taxes and utilities of 1.1 per cent, and depreciation rate of 1.1 per cent, using data covering almost all properties advertized for rent in major Australian cities. This gives us a benchmark net rent-price ratio of 0.02. Applying the rent-price approach to this benchmark gives us the unadjusted long-run net rent-price ratio series depicted as orange circles in in Figure A.5. We make one adjustment to these series to correct for possible mismeasurement of rental growth when lifting the wartime price controls in 1949/50 (see below for details). This gives us the adjusted final rent-price ratio series—the green-circled line in Figure A.5—used in this paper.

We obtain several scattered independent estimates of rent-price ratios in Australia. First, the IPD database (MSCI, 2016) reports a net rent-price ratio of 0.032 for the Australian residential real estate in 2013 (black square in Figure A.5). Balance sheet approach estimates (brown triangles) are obtained using a variety of sources. OECD (2016b), Stapledon (2007), Australian Bureau of Statistics (2014) and Butlin (1985) provide estimates of gross rental expenditure and various maintenance and running costs, as well as depreciation, for present-day and historical periods. As with the benchmark yield calculation, we subtract all non-tax and non-utilities related running costs, plus depreciation, to calculate total net rental expenditure. We then combine it with the housing wealth data from Stapledon (2007) and Piketty and Zucman (2014) to calculate the net rental yield.

The historical balance-sheet approach estimates are broadly in line with the unadjusted rent-price approach series (orange circles) over recent decades, but below it for the earlier years. Note that the long-run rent-price ratio shows a structural break in 1949/1950 stemming from a surge in house prices after the lifting of wartime price controls in 1949 (price controls for houses and land were introduced in 1942). While the abandonment of price controls undoubtedly had an effect on house prices, it is unclear whether it also resulted in a single sudden shift in the relationship between house prices and rents. To guard against measurement uncertainty, we benchmark our historical rent-price ratio to the balance sheet approach estimate in 1949. Figure A.5 shows that the adjusted long-run rent price ratio—the green circle line—generally concords with the balance-sheet approach estimates, being on average slightly lower during 1900–1940, and higher during 1950–1980.

Finally, modern-day gross rental yield estimates are available from Numbeo.com for one- and three-bedroom apartments i). within city-centres and ii). in the rest of the country. We adjust these down using the cost estimates from Fox and Tulip (2014) to obtain a proxy of net yield. The resulting estimates fall in-between those of the MSCI (2016), and the other approaches.

Belgium

Figure A.6: *Belgium: plausibility of rent-price ratio*

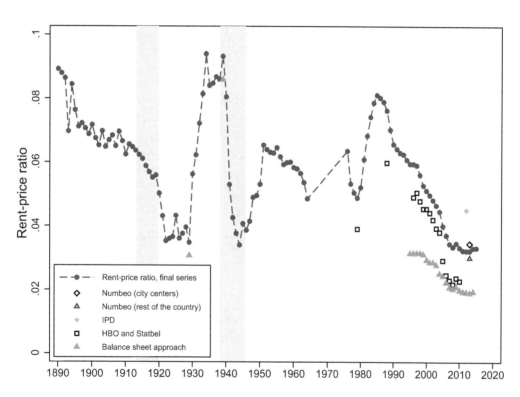

We construct the benchmark rent-price ratio using the rental yield data from Numbeo.com, taking the average of in- and out-of-city-centre apartments, and adjusting down one-third to account for running costs and depreciation. This gives us a benchmark net rent-price ratio of 0.033 for 2012. Applying the rent-price approach gives us the long-run net rent-price ratio series depicted as green circles in Figure A.6, which are the estimates used in this paper. Please note that the benchmark rent-price ratio from the IPD (MSCI, 2016)—0.045 for 2012—is substantially higher than the alternative approaches, which is why we rely on estimates from Numbeo.com instead.

We construct four independent estimates of rent-price ratios. First, for 1978–2010, Statistics Belgium publish estimates of average rental expenditure and house prices (Statistics Belgium, 2013b, 2015). Assuming around one-third of gross rent is spent on maintenance, running costs and depreciation, this gives us a series of net rent-price ratios, depicted as square dots in Figure A.6.

The resulting series are consistent with both the level and the time trend in our baseline series constructed using the rent-price approach.

Second, we construct estimates of gross rent-price ratios using the balance-sheet approach, based on data on rental expenditure and housing wealth, and scale these down one-third to obtain the net yield proxy. For the modern period, Poullet (2013) provides estimates of housing wealth, and Statistics Belgium (2013a) and OECD (2016b) of rental expenditure. For historical series, Peeters, Goossens, and Buyst (2005) reports estimates of total gross and net rents on all dwellings, which we scale down to obtain an estimate of net rental expenditure on residential real estate. Goldsmith and Frijdal (1975) report estimates of housing wealth for 1948–1971, which we extend back to 1929 using data in Goldsmith (1985), and assuming a constant share of land to residential property value. The resulting net rental yield estimates are somewhat below our baseline rent-price ratio for the modern period, and broadly in line with its historical levels, falling within a reasonable margin of error given the substantial uncertainty in the Belgian housing wealth estimates.

We would like to thank Stijn Van Nieuwerburgh for sharing historical rent and house price data for Belgium.

Denmark

Figure A.7: *Denmark: plausibility of rent-price ratio*

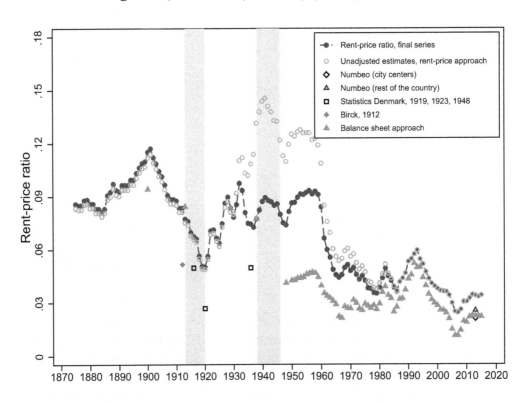

For 2013, the MSCI (2016) reports the rent-price ratio for Danish residential real estate of 0.034. Applying the rent-price approach to this benchmark gives us the unadjusted long-run net rent-price ratio series depicted as orange circles in in Figure A.7. We make one adjustment to these series to correct for possible mismeasurement of rental growth around World War 2 (see below for details).

This gives us the final adjusted rent-price ratio series—the green-circled line in Figure A.7—used in this paper.

We obtain several additional estimates of rent-price ratios in Denmark throughout the past century and a half. First, we construct estimates using the balance sheet approach using data on total rental expenditure (Hansen, 1976; OECD, 2016b; Statistics Denmark, 2017b) and housing wealth (Abildgren, 2016). We estimate housing running costs and depreciation as fixed proportions of dwelling intermediate consumption, and depreciation of all buildings (Statistics Denmark, 2017a), and subtract these from gross rental expenditure to produce net rental yield estimates. The balance sheet approach yields are similar to the rent-price approach for the recent decades and in the early 20th century, but diverge somewhat in the 1940s and 50s. Both estimates are subject to measurement error, but the large difference suggests that some of the high levels of the rent-price approach ratio may be a result of the rental index underestimating the rent growth during this period. To guard against accumulation of errors in the rent-price approach, we benchmark the historical yield to the balance sheet approach estimates in 1938 and 1929, and adjust the rent-price ratio growth for the in-between years, with the final series (green circles) being somewhere in-between the balance-sheet and rent-price approaches. For earlier the historical period, the rent-price and balance-sheet approaches display similar levels and time trend.

Our baseline rent-price ratio estimates are also in line with two further historical sources. First, according to Birck (1912), at the time of his writing, housing values in Copenhagen typically amounted to 13 times the annual rental income. Second, in line with this estimate, Statistics Denmark (1919) reports that housing values in urban areas in 1916 were about 13.5 times the annual rental income (note that housing values reported in Statistics Denmark (1919, 1923, 1948, 1954) relate to valuation for tax purposes). These data imply a gross rent-price ratio of about 0.06–0.07, and a net rent-price ratio of around 0.04–0.05. For 1920, Statistics Denmark (1923) states that housing values in urban areas were about 25 times the annual rental income implying a gross rent-price ratio of roughly 0.04 (roughly 0.03 net). In 1936, rent-price ratios in urban areas had returned to pre-World War 1 levels (Statistics Denmark, 1948). Finally, estimates of net rent-price ratios based on data from www.Numbeo.com are similar to the modern-day values for the balance-sheet and rent-price approaches.

Finland

Figure A.8: *Finland: plausibility of rent-price ratio*

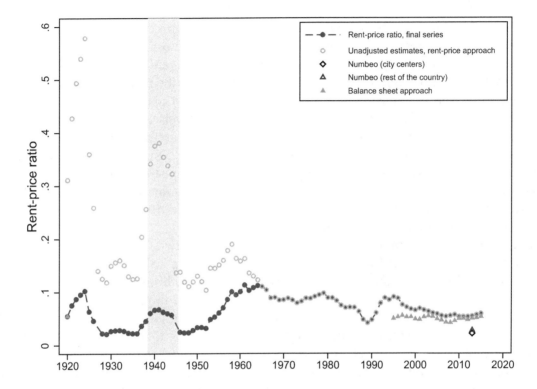

For 2013, the MSCI (2016) reports the rent-price ratio for Finnish residential real estate of 0.054. Applying the rent-price approach to this benchmark gives us the unadjusted long-run net rent-price ratio series depicted as orange circles in in Figure A.8. We make one adjustment to these series to correct for possible mismeasurement of rental growth during the rent controls imposed in the early-to-mid 20th century (see below for details). This gives us the final adjusted rent-price ratio series—the green-circled line in Figure A.8—used in this paper.

We obtain two alternative estimates of the net rent-price ratio for the modern period. First, we construct proxies of gross rental expenditure, running costs and depreciation, and total housing wealth back to 1995 using data from Statistics Finland and OECD. These are roughly the same as our benchmark rent-price ratio for the benchmark year, but are slightly lower in the late 1990s. Note, however, that data from Statistics Finland imply a housing depreciation rate of 3.5%, and running and maintenance costs of around 2%, which corresponds to an expected duration of the structure of less than 20 years. Therefore, the cost estimates are almost certainly too high, and adjusting these to more reasonable levels would leave the rent-price ratios on par, or above our baseline values. For 2013, we also obtain estimates of rent-price ratios for one- and three-bedroom apartments i) within city-centers and ii) in the rest of the country from www.Numbeo.com. Once adjusted for costs, these are somewhat lower than both the estimates using the rent-price and balance sheet approach.

We also construct an independent estimate of the rent-price ratio in Finland in 1920 using data on total housing value (Statistics Finland, 1920) and total expenditure on rents (Hjerppe, 1989), adjusted down by one-third to account for running costs and depreciation. Figure A.8 shows that this estimate is significantly below the long-run rent price ratio in 1920. Similarly to the case of Spain, the discrepancy between the rent-price approach and alternative estimates may reflect difficulties of the Finnish statistical office to construct a rent index after the introduction of wartime rent controls. Rent controls were introduced during WW2 and were only abolished under the *Tenancy Act* of 1961 (Whitehead, 2012). While this period of deregulation was rather short-lived—rent regulation was re-introduced in 1968 and parts of the private rental market were subject to rent regulation until the mid-1990s—the downward trend of the long-run rent-price ratio appears particularly remarkable. In other words, the data suggest that rents during the period of deregulation increased significantly less than house prices. To the best of our knowledge, no quantitative or qualitative evidence exists supporting such a pronounced fall in the rent-price ratio during the first half of the 1960s. We therefore conjecture that the rent index suffers from a downward bias during the period of wartime rent regulation and immediately thereafter. To mitigate this bias, we adjust the gross growth rate in rents between WW2 and 1965 up by a constant factor calibrated so that the adjusted long-run rent-price ratio concords with the independent estimate in 1920, which is a factor of 1.1. Figure A.8 displays the resulting adjusted long-run rent-price ratio.

France

Figure A.9: *France: plausibility of rent-price ratio*

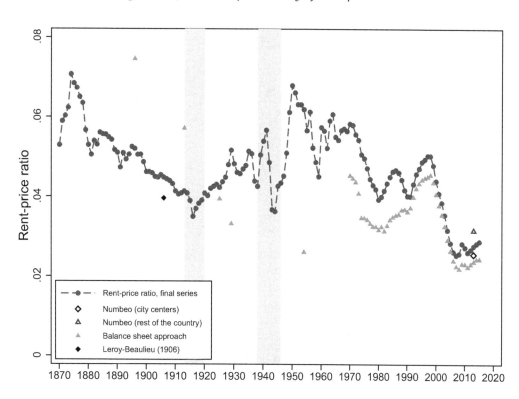

For 2013, the MSCI (2016) reports the rent-price ratio for French residential real estate of 0.028. Applying the rent-price approach to this benchmark gives us the long-run net rent-price ratio series depicted as green circles in in Figure A.9, which are the estimates used in this paper.

We obtain several scattered independent estimates of rent-price ratios in France since 1870. First, we calculate rent-price ratios using the balance-sheet approach, based on the data on total housing value (Piketty and Zucman, 2014) and total expenditure on rents (Statistics France, 2016b; Villa, 1994) net of running costs and depreciation (Piketty and Zucman, 2014; Statistics France, 2016a,b).

These estimates are in line with those using the rent-price approach, even though the balance-sheet approach rental yield estimates for 1900–1920 are somewhat higher, and for 1920–1960 somewhat lower. Second, `Numbeo.com` estimates of modern-day rent-price ratios are in line with the IPD benchmark.

A few additional scattered estimates on housing returns for the pre-WW2 period are available. For 1903, Haynie (1903) reports an average gross rental yield for Paris of about 4 percent. For 1906, Leroy-Beaulieu (1906) estimates a gross rental yield for Paris of 6.36 percent, ranging from 5.13 percent in the 16th arrondissement to 7.76 percent in the 20th arrondissement. Simonnet, Gallais-Hamonno, and Arbulu (1998) state that the gross rent of residential properties purchased by the property investment fund *La Fourmi Immobiliere* amounted to about 6 to 7 percent of property value between 1899 and 1913. These estimates are generally comparable with an average annual net rental yield of about 5 percent for 1914–1938 for the final series used in this paper.

Germany

Figure A.10: *Germany: plausibility of rent-price ratio*

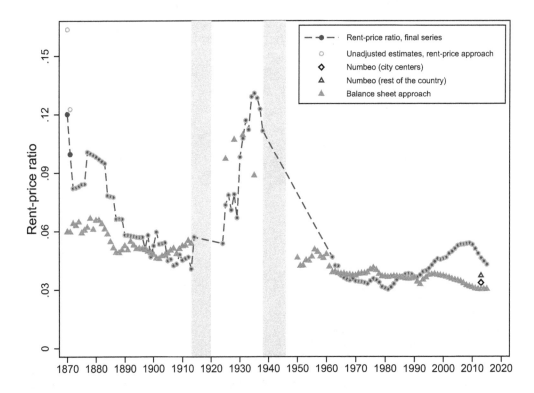

For 2013, the MSCI (2016) reports the rent-price ratio for German residential real estate of 0.047. Applying the rent-price approach to this benchmark gives us the unadjusted long-run net rent-price ratio series depicted as orange circles in in Figure A.10. We make one adjustment to these series to correct for possible mismeasurement of rental growth in the early 1870s (see below for details). This gives us the final adjusted rent-price ratio series—the green-circled line in Figure A.10—used in this paper.

We obtain three independent estimates of historical rent-price ratios in Germany. First, `Numbeo.com` estimates of modern-day rent-price ratios are broadly in line with the rent-price approach.

Second, we calculate the balance sheet approach estimates for benchmark years based on data on total housing value and total expenditure on rents. The housing wealth series combines the data in Piketty and Zucman (2014), and various issues of *Statistik der Einheitswerte*. For the pre-WW1 period, we scale up the value of structures reported in Piketty and Zucman (2014) to obtain a proxy for total housing wealth. The rental expenditure data are from OECD (2016b) and Statistics Germany (2013) for the modern period, and (Hoffmann, 1965) for the period before WW2. Throughout we assume around one-third of gross rent is spent on costs and depreciation to obtain a proxy for net rental expenditure.

Figure A.10 shows that the balance sheet approach estimates confirm the general level and historical time trend of the rent-price ratio: rents were high in the interwar period, and comparatively lower before WW1 and after WW2. The modern-day balance sheet approach estimates are somewhat below those in our final series, but within a reasonable margin of error, given the uncertainty in estimating housing wealth, imputed rents, running costs and depreciation. For the years 1870–1871, however, the balance sheet approach estimates of rental yield are relatively stable, whereas those using the rent-price approach are markedly high. It is likely that the rental index underestimated the rental growth during years 1870–1871, when house prices grew sharply. However, the balance sheet approach net yield estimate is in itself highly uncertain, as housing wealth data may have been smoothed over time, and there is little data on the value of land underlying dwellings. We therefore adjust the rental yield down to the average of the rent-price figures, and an alternative rental yield series that extrapolates the growth of rents back using the balance sheet approach. This results in the green dots, our final series for 1870–1871, that suggests that rental yields fell during those years, but probably by less than suggested by the raw unadjusted series.

Finally, one additional series on housing returns is available for the pre-WW2 period. For 1870–1913, Tilly (1986) reports housing returns for Germany and Berlin. Average annual real net returns according to Tilly (1986) amount to about 8 percent—a figure similar to the circa 10 percent p.a. average annual real return calculated using the adjusted rent and house price data.

Figure A.11: *Italy: plausibility of rent-price ratio*

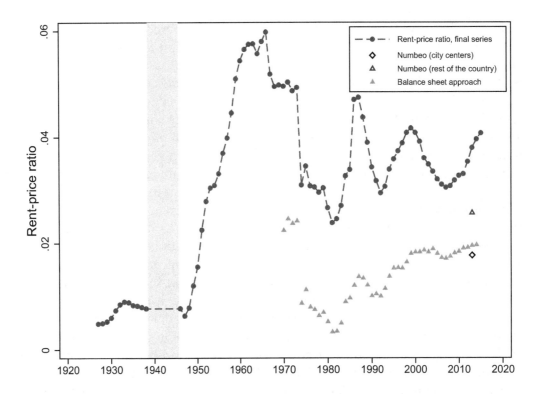

For 2013, the MSCI (2016) reports the rent-price ratio for Italian residential real estate of 0.038. Applying the rent-price approach to this benchmark gives us the long-run net rent-price ratio series depicted as green circles in in Figure A.11, which are the estimates used in this paper.

To gauge the plausibility of historical rent-price ratios, we construct the balance-sheet approach rental yields as total rental expenditure net or running costs and depreciation, in proportion to total housing wealth (Istat, 2016; Piketty and Zucman, 2014). These are somewhat lower than the rent-price approach estimate, but confirm the general trend in the rent-price ratio from the 1970s onwards. Finally, Numbeo.com estimates of modern-day rent-price ratios are similar to the rent-price and balance sheet approach.

Japan

Figure A.12: *Japan: plausibility of rent-price ratio*

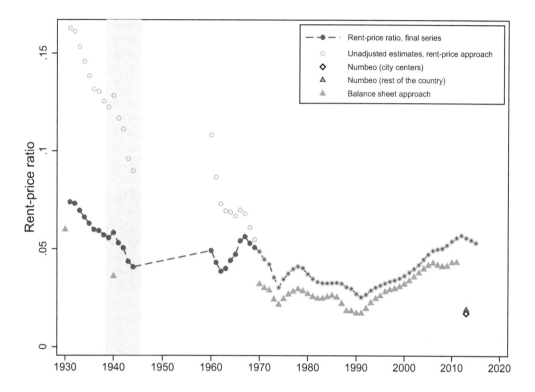

For 2013, the MSCI (2016) reports the rent-price ratio for Japanese residential real estate of 0.056. Applying the rent-price approach to this benchmark gives us the unadjusted long-run net rent-price ratio series depicted as orange circles in in Figure A.12. We make one adjustment to these series to correct for possible mismeasurement of rental growth in the 1960s (see below for details). This gives us the final adjusted rent-price ratio series—the green-circled line in Figure A.12—used in this paper.

We obtain two independent estimates for rent-price ratios in Japan. First, we calculate rent-price ratios for benchmark years (1930, 1940, 1970–2011) based on data on total housing value (Goldsmith, 1985; Piketty and Zucman, 2014) and total expenditure on rents (Cabinet Office. Government of Japan, 2012; Shinohara, 1967). To proxy the net rent-price ratio, we assume around one-third of gross rent is spent on running costs and depreciation. The resulting estimates are consistent with the long-run rent-price ratio for the period 1970–2011 (Figure A.12). Yet, for 1930 and 1940 the estimates are much lower than those using the rent-price approach. This suggests that the rent index may have underestimated rent growth between 1940 and 1970, thus inflating the historical rental yield estimates. Indeed, the unadjusted series imply that the rent-price ratio fell dramatically during the 1970s, a trend not mirrored in any subsequent period, or in the balance-sheet approach data. To this end, we conjecture that the rental index understated the growth in rents by a factor of two during the 1960s. The resulting adjusted rent-price ratio (green circles) is then consistent with the historical estimates using the balance sheet approach.

Second, estimates of modern-day rent-price ratios from Numbeo.com are are somewhat below both the rent-price approach and balance-sheet approach estimates for the 2010s.

Netherlands

Figure A.13: *Netherlands: plausibility of rent-price ratio*

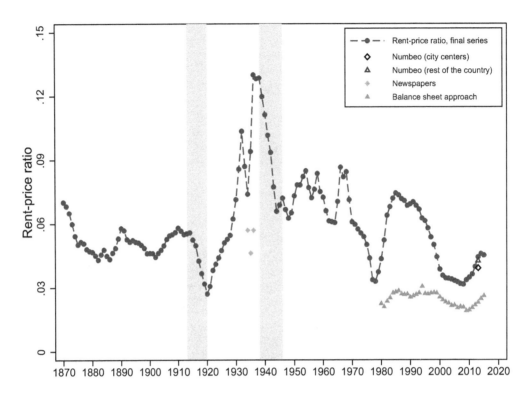

For 2013, the MSCI (2016) reports the rent-price ratio for Dutch residential real estate of 0.044. Applying the rent-price approach to this benchmark gives us the long-run net rent-price ratio series depicted as green circles in in Figure A.13, which are the estimates used in this paper.

We obtain two independent estimates for rent-price ratios in the Netherlands. First, we calculate the rent-price ratio using the balance sheet approach, based on estimates of rental expenditure from OECD (2016b), and housing wealth estimated from non-financial balance sheet data in OECD (2016c) and Groote, Albers, and De Jong (1996) (brown trianges in Figure A.13). We assume one-third of gross rental is spent on running costs and depreciation. The yields confirm the general trend in our benchmark series, although their levels are somewhat lower. It is worth noting that the estimates of housing wealth and running costs for the Netherlands are highly uncertain, hence we do not put too much weight on the level of the balance-sheet approach yields.

Second, a number of newspaper advertisements and articles in the mid-1930s report rent-price ratio levels of 0.07-0.09, which we conjecture are around 0.05 - 0.06 in net terms, once running costs and depreciation are taken out (Limburgsch Dagblad, 1935; Nieuwe Tilburgsche Courant, 1934, 1936). These are somewhat lower than our baseline series, but similar to the levels observed in the early 1930s, with the remaining margin of error easily attributed to location specificity (the advertisements are for city-center properties, with the correspondingly lower yiedls). More generally, residential real estate was perceived as a highly profitable investment throughout the decade (De Telegraaf, 1939). Finally, estimates of the rent-price ratio based on data from Numbeo.com are almost identical to our baseline IPD benchmark (MSCI, 2016).

Norway

Figure A.14: *Norway: plausibility of rent-price ratio*

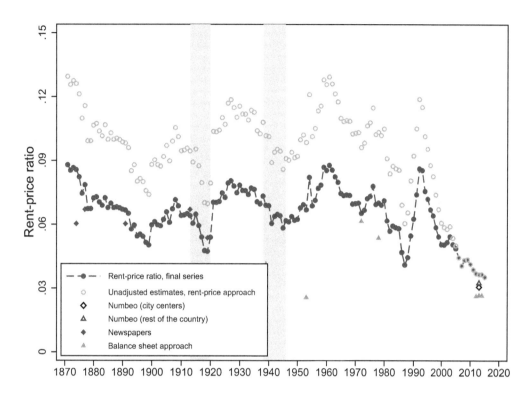

For 2013, the MSCI (2016) reports the rent-price ratio for Norwegian residential real estate of 0.037. Applying the rent-price approach to this benchmark gives us the unadjusted long-run net rent-price ratio series depicted as orange circles in in Figure A.14. We make one adjustment to these series to bring the estimates in line with alternative historical sources (see below for details). This gives us the final adjusted rent-price ratio series—the green-circled line in Figure A.14—used in this paper.

We obtain several scattered independent estimates of rent-price ratios in Norway since 1871. First, we calculate rent-price ratios for benchmark years using the balance-sheet approach, based on data on total housing value (Goldsmith, 1985; OECD, 2016c) and total expenditure on rents (OECD, 2016b; Statistics Norway, 1954, 2014), and assuming one-third of gross rent is consumed by running costs and depreciation expenses to estimate the net rental yield. Note that for the historical expenditure series, we estimate rents as 80% of total housing expenditure, a proportion consistent with modern-day Norwegian data, and historical data for the US. We also collect scattered data from advertisements for Oslo residential real estate in *Aftenposten*, one of Norway's largest newspapers, with the gross advertised yield again adjusted down by one-third to proxy the net figure.

Both these sets of estimates confirm the general long-run trend in the rent-price ratio. The long-run rent-price ratio was essentially stable up until the early 2000s, with increases in early 20th century and late 1960s reversed by falls in World War 1 and the 1980s, and is currently at a historical low. However the long-run level of the ratio is generally lower than the estimates using the rent-price approach (orange diamonds): around 6%–8% rather than 8%–12%, and this divergence is already apparent in the late 1970s. Based on this, we stipulate that the rental index during late 1990s and early 2000s—a period when house prices increased substantially—understated the growth of rents relative to prices, leading the rent-price approach to overstate the historical rental yields. To correct for this presumed bias, we adjust the growth in rents up by a factor of 1.5 for the years 1990 to 2005. The resulting adjusted rent-price ratio (green circles) is in line with the historical estimates both in terms of levels and trend.

Lastly, estimates of the rent-price ratio based on data from www.Numbeo.com are in line with our baseline IPD benchmark (MSCI, 2016).

Portugal

Figure A.15: *Portugal: plausibility of rent-price ratio*

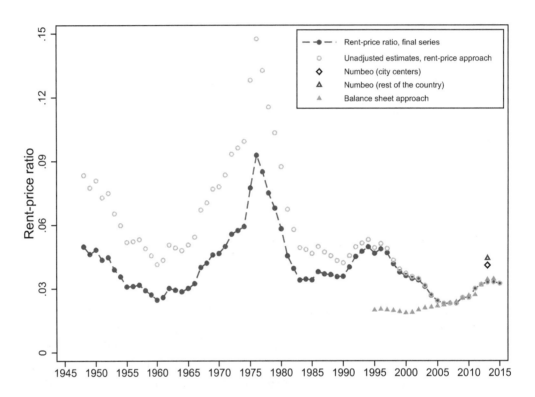

For 2013, the MSCI (2016) reports the rent-price ratio for Portuguese residential real estate of 0.033. Applying the rent-price approach to this benchmark gives us the unadjusted long-run net rent-price ratio series depicted as orange circles in in Figure A.15. We make one adjustment to these series to correct for potential biases arising from rent mismeasurement during the prolonged period of rent controls in the last quarter of the 20th century (see below for details). This gives us the final adjusted rent-price ratio series—the green-circled line in Figure A.15—used in this paper.

We obtain several scattered independent estimates of rent-price ratios in Portugal. First, estimates of the rent-price ratio based on data from www.Numbeo.com are slightly above, but broadly in line with our baseline IPD benchmark (MSCI, 2016). Second, we compute the rental yield using the balance-sheet approach, based on data on total rental expenditure (OECD, 2016b) and total housing wealth (Cardoso, Farinha, and Lameira, 2008), scaled down one-third to adjust for running costs and depreciation. These are almost identical to the rent-price approach for the recent years, but diverge somewhat in the late 1990s. More generally, the historical growth in rents relative to house prices in Portugal may have been understated due to the imposition of rent controls in 1974, which remained in place in various forms until well into the 2000s. This seems likely given the high levels of the unadjusted rent-price approach yields in the 1970s and early 1980s (orange circles in Figure A.15). Unfortunately, no alternative historical estimates of the rent-price ratio before 1995 are available for Portugal. Instead, we stipulate that the rent-price ratio in the 1940s and 50s, before the reported high rent inflation of the 1960s (Cardoso, 1983) and the subsequent rent controls, was at levels similar to the 1980s and 1990s. To achieve that, we adjust rental growth up by a factor of 1.2 for years 1974–2005; the period for which rent controls were in place.

The resulting adjusted long-run rent-price ratio (green circles in Figure A.15) concords with the narrative evidence on house prices and rent developments in Portugal. Real house prices in Portugal rose after the end of WW2 until the Carnation Revolution in 1974. After a brief but substantial house price recession after the revolution, real house prices embarked on a steep incline (Azevedo, 2016). By contrast, real rents remained broadly stable between 1948 and the mid-1960s as well as after 1990 but exhibit a pronounced boom and bust pattern between the mid-1960s and the mid-1980s. According to Cardoso (1983), the rapid growth of inflation-adjusted rents between the mid-1960s and the mid-1970s was the result of both rising construction costs and high inflation expectations. In 1974, new rent legislation provided for a rent freeze on existing contracts. Rent increases were also regulated between tenancies but unregulated for new construction. These regulations resulted in lower rent growth rates and rents considerably lagging behind inflation (Cardoso, 1983), and a consequent fall in the rent-price ratio.

Spain

Figure A.16: *Spain: plausibility of rent-price ratio*

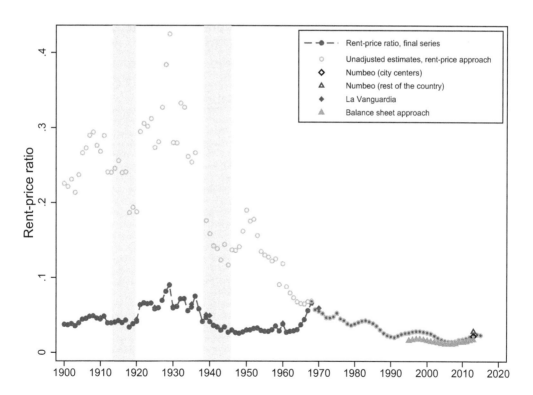

For 2013, the MSCI (2016) reports the rent-price ratio for Spanish residential real estate of 0.025. Applying the rent-price approach to this benchmark gives us the unadjusted long-run net rent-price ratio series depicted as orange circles in in Figure A.16. We make one adjustment to these series to correct for possible mismeasurement of rental growth during the rent controls imposed in the early-to-mid 20th century (see below for details). This gives us the final adjusted rent-price ratio series—the green-circled line in Figure A.16—used in this paper.

We obtain several scattered independent estimates of rent-price ratios in Spain. First, estimates of the rent-price ratio based on data from www.Numbeo.com are almost identical to our baseline IPD benchmark (MSCI, 2016). Second, we construct net rent-price ratios using the balance sheet approach, as total rental expenditure (OECD, 2016b) less running costs and depreciation (assumed to be one-third of gross rent), in relation to housing wealth (Artola Blanco, Bauluz, and Martínez-Toledano, 2017). These are slightly below but broadly in line with the rent-price approach for the overlapping years.

Finally, we collected scattered data on rent-price ratios from advertisements for Barcelona residential real estate in *La Vanguardia* for benchmark years (1910, 1914, 1920, 1925, 1930, 1935, 1940, 1950, 1960, 1970). For each of the benchmark years, we construct an average rent-price ratio based on between 25 and 46 advertisements. The gross ratios in the advertisements are adjusted down to exclude running costs and depreciation, calibrated at 2% p.a., around one-third of the advertized yields. Figure A.16 shows that the newspaper estimates are significantly below the rent-price ratio for the benchmark years between 1910 and 1960. Yet it also suggests that rent-price ratios were generally higher before the mid-1950s. Similarly to Finland, this trajectory may reflect difficulties of the Spanish statistical office to construct a rent index after the introduction of rent freezes in the 1930s and during the years of strong rent regulation after WW2. While the rent freeze was lifted in 1945, these regulations remained effective until the mid-1960s. Specifically, the data suggest that rents between the end of WW2 and the mid-1960s increased substantially less than house prices. To the best of our knowledge, no quantitative or qualitative evidence exists supporting such a pronounced fall in the rent-price ratio in the immediate post-WW2 years or a generally higher level of rental yields prior to the 1960s. To mitigate this bias, we adjust the growth rate in rents between 1910 and 1960 so that the adjusted long-run rent-price ratio concords with the independent estimates obtained from *La Vanguardia*. Figure A.16 displays the resulting adjusted long-run rent-price ratio (green circles), which is the final series we use in this paper.

Sweden

Figure A.17: *Sweden: plausibility of rent-price ratio*

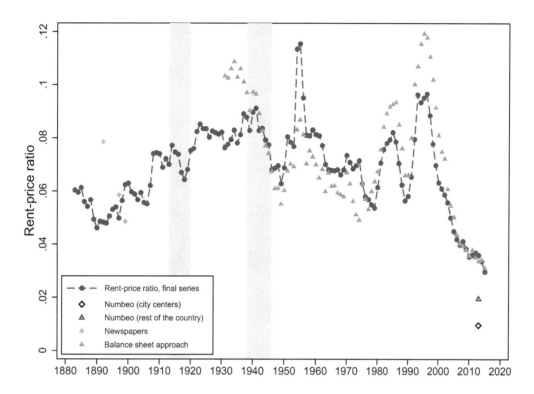

For 2013, the MSCI (2016) reports the rent-price ratio for Swedish residential real estate of 0.036. Applying the rent-price approach to this benchmark gives us the long-run net rent-price ratio series depicted as green circles in in Figure A.17, which are the estimates used in this paper.

We obtain three independent estimates of rent-price ratios for Sweden. First, we compute net rental yields based on the balance-sheet approach as total rental expenditure less running costs and depreciation, as a share of housing wealth, drawing on a variety of sources. The modern-day rental expenditure data are obtained from OECD (2016b), and further data back to 1969 were provided by Birgitta Magnusson Wärmark at Statistics Sweden. These are extrapolated back to 1931 using data on total housing expenditure from Dahlman and Klevmarken (1971). The data on running costs are a weighted average of total repairs of dwellings (data provided by Jonas Zeed at Statistics Sweden), and maintenance costs on rentals reported by (OECD, 2016b) scaled up to capture owner-occupied dwellings. Data on depreciation were provided by Jonas Zeed at Statistics Sweden, and were extrapolated back using dwellings depreciation in Edvinsson (2016). Before 1995, running costs are assumed to have evolved in line with depreciation. The long-run housing wealth data are sourced from Waldenström (2017). Both the level and the time trend in the resulting long-run rent-price ratio are in line with the historical balance-sheet approach estimates.

Second, the rent-price ratio in the late 19th / early 20th century is in line with those reported in several newspaper advertisements and articles. According to these sources, gross rent-price ratios were in the range of 0.07 to 0.1, and residential real estate was perceived as highly profitable investment (Dagens Nyheter, 1892, 1897, 1899). Given that running costs and depreciation amounted to around 2% p.a. of property value in Sweden during the period 1930–2015, this leads us to conjecture that net rent-price ratios were around 0.05–0.08, in line with our estimates.

Finally, estimates of modern-day rent-price ratios from Numbeo.com are somewhat below both our benchmark ratio and the balance sheet approach. However these are not based on a representative or matched sample of properties for sale and for rent, and are therefore less reliable than the alternative estimates.

Switzerland

Figure A.18: *Switzerland: plausibility of rent-price ratio*

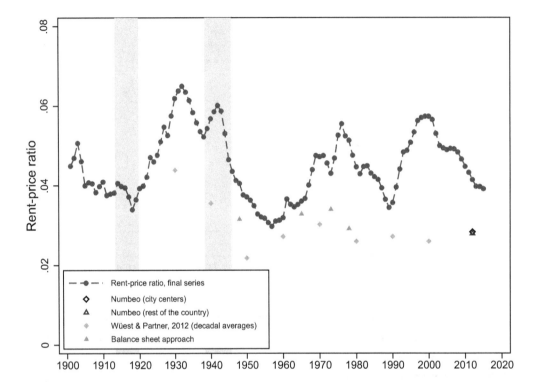

For 2013, the MSCI (2016) reports the rent-price ratio for Swiss residential real estate of 0.040. Applying the rent-price approach to this benchmark gives us the long-run net rent-price ratio series depicted as green circles in in Figure A.18, which are the estimates used in this paper.

To check the plausibility of the long-run rent-price ratio, we obtain four independent estimates. First, Real (1950) reports real returns on residential real estate in Zurich of 6 percent in 1927 and 7.3 percent in 1933. These data are—by and large—in line with the estimates of housing returns constructed by merging the indices of house prices and rents. Second, West and Partner (2012) estimate 10-year averages of real rental yields in Switzerland for 1920–2000. Assuming around one-third of gross rent goes to running costs and depreciation, the resulting net rental yield estiamtes are broadly consistent with the long-run rent-price ratio (Figure A.18), taking into account the various estimation uncertainties. For the post-World War 2 period, we calculate rent-price ratios using the balance sheet approach for benchmark years (1948, 1965, 1973, 1978) drawing on data on housing wealth from Goldsmith (1985), rental expenditure from Statistics Switzerland (2014), and assuming one-third of gross rent is taken up by runnign costs and depreciation. Again, the resulting estimates are broadly consistent with the long-run rent-price ratio (Figure A.18).

Finally, estimates of rent-price ratios based on data from Numbeo.com are somewhat below, but within a reasonable error margin of the MSCI (2016) benchmark ratio.

United Kingdom

Figure A.19: *United Kingdom: plausibility of rent-price ratio*

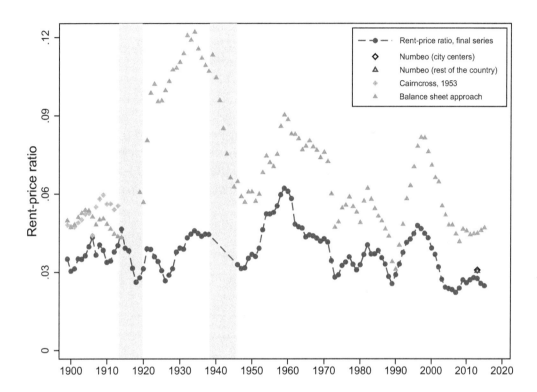

For 2013, the MSCI (2016) reports the rent-price ratio for U.K. residential real estate of 0.032. Applying the rent-price approach to this benchmark gives us the long-run net rent-price ratio series depicted as green circles in in Figure A.19, which are the estimates used in this paper. Please note that for years 1947–1955, no rental index data were available, and we extrapolated the rent-price ratio series using the growth in the "balance sheet approach" measure, benchmarking against rental index values in 1946 and 1956.[26]

We construct several alternative estimates of the rent-price ratio for the period going back to 1900. First, we construct the net rental yield based on the balance-sheet approach using data on total rental expenditure less running costs and depreciation, in proportion to housing wealth, based on a variety of sources. For rents, we rely on historical series of housing and rental expenditure from Mitchell (1988), Sefton and Weale (1995) and Piketty and Zucman (2014), combined with recent Office for National Statistics (ONS) data, and historical data from the ONS shared with us by Amanda Bell. Estimates of costs and depreciation are available from the UK National Accounts, and housing wealth is taken from Piketty and Zucman (2014). It is worth noting that the estimates of rental expenditure for the UK are subject to large uncertainty: the ONS updated the methodology

---

[26]We assume that the 1956 index value is correct, but correct the 1946 rental index value for possible biases arising from the wartime rent controls, such that the trend in the rent-price ratios matches that in the balance sheet approach measure, and the 1956 rent-price approach estimate.

for rent imputation in 2016, resulting in large upward revisions to historical imputed rent estimates (by as large as a factor of three). It is possible that some of the historical data are subject to similar uncertainties, which helps explain why the rental yield levels using the balance sheet approach are so much higher than the extrapolated rent-price ratio, even though the time trend is similar.

Some additional scattered data on rent-price ratios are available for the pre-WW2 period. For England, Cairncross (1975) reports an average gross rent-price ratio of 0.068 between 1895 and 1913, or around 0.05 in net terms. Offer (1981) estimates slightly higher rent-price ratios for selected years between 1892 and 1913 for occupied leasehold dwellings in London. As Figure A.19 shows, these data are slightly higher, but broadly consistent with the our long-run rent-price ratio estimates (an average of 0.037 during 1900–1913). Tarbuck (1938) states that high-quality freehold houses were valued at 25 to 16 years purchase and lower quality freehold houses at 14 to 11 years purchase in the 1930s, again broadly consistent with our estimates.

Overall, these estimates suggest that our rental yields for the UK are somewhat conservative, but fit the time pattern and broad levels found in the alternative historical sources.

Concerning the modern period, estimates of the rent-price ratio based on data from www.Numbeo.com are very similar to the MSCI (2016) benchmark. Additionally, Bracke (2015) estimates a gross rental yield of 0.05 on central London properties over the period 2006–2012, based on a matched micro-level dataset of around 2000 properties. Again, these estimates are consistent with our data.

United States

Figure A.20: *United States: plausibility of rent-price ratio*

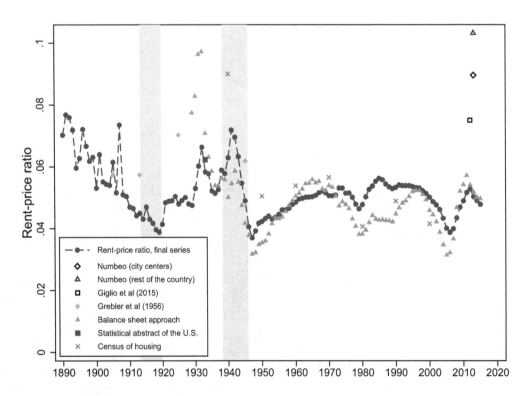

For 2014, the MSCI (2016) reports the rent-price ratio for U.S. residential real estate of 0.049. Applying the rent-price approach to this benchmark gives us the long-run net rent-price ratio series depicted as green circles in in Figure A.20, which are the estimates used in this paper.

We obtain independent estimates of U.S. rent-price ratios from five additional sources. First, decadal averages of gross price-rent ratios are available for 1899–1938 from Grebler, Blank, and Winnick (1956) ranging between 10.4 and 12.6. Second, estimates of gross rents paid and home values are available from various issues of the U.S. Census and Statistical Abstract, published by U.S. Census Bureau (1942, 2013). Once adjusted for estimates of running costs and depreciation, the estimates from these sources are similar to the price-rent ratios resulting from merging the indices of house prices and rents (see Figure A.20). Third, we calculate the rent-price ratio using the balance sheet approach, as total rental expenditure less housing running costs—estimated as 2/3 of total housing intermediate consumption—in proportion to total housing value, using expenditure data from Bureau of Economic Analysis (2014) and housing wealth estimates in Saez and Zucman (2016). Reassuringly, the resulting estimates are very close to the long-run rent-price ratio. Estimates of the rent-price ratio for 2012 are also available from the real estate portal Trulia, as used by Giglio, Maggiori, and Stroebel (2015). The resulting net rent-price ratio of 0.075 is higher than the figures from MSCI (2016) and the balance sheet approach. This may be because the Trulia ratios are not market cap weighted, and may overweigh the high-yield low-housing-wealth areas outside of cities. Alternatively, the MSCI (2016) IPD ratio could understate the rental yield because investor portfolios tend to be concentrated in cities. To be consistent with the balance sheet approach and to remain conservative, we use the IPD ratio as our benchmark.

Finally, estimates of the rent-price ratio based on data from www.Numbeo.com are higher than our benchmark estimate and similar to the Trulia transaction-level data. As with the Trulia data, these are not market-capitalization weighted, which may bias the rental yield estimates upwards. Given the similarity to the balance-sheet approach yields and the historical estimates from Grebler, Blank, and Winnick (1956), the rent-price approach estimates stemming from the MSCI (2016) benchmark should provide the most accurate picture of the historical rental returns on housing in the US. Still, given the higher alternative benchmark yield estimates of Trulia and Numbeo.com, our housing return series for the US should be viewed as conservative compared to other possible alternatives.

L. Equity and bond returns

This section details the sources used to construct the total equity and bond return series in this paper.

Australia

Table A.16: *Data sources: equity and bond returns, Australia*

Year	Data source
Equity returns:	
1870–1881	Sum of capital gains, dividends and gains or losses from stock operations for Australian shares listed in London, weighted by market capitalization. Constructed from *Investor Monthly Manual* (IMM) data, various issues (http://som.yale.edu/imm-issues).
1882–2008	With-dividend return from Brailsford, Handley, and Maheswaran (2012). Note: we use these series rather than the alternative from NERA Economic Consulting (2015) due to greater consistency with the IMM historical series.
2009–2013	Total equity return from NERA Economic Consulting (2015).
2014–2015	MSCI total return index
Bond returns:	
1900–1925	Total return on Australian government bonds listed in Sydney from Moore (2010b). Converted from pound sterling to Australian Dollar.
1926–1968	Total return on Australian bonds listed in London. Data for 1926–1929 are from Meyer, Reinhart, and Trebesch (2015), shared by Josefin Meyer. Data for 1930–1968 were constructed by the authors.
1969–1987	Implied capital gain + yield from the 10-year government bond yield series published by the Reserve Bank of Australia. Capital gain estimated from movements in yields, using monthly yield data. Spliced with London listings data over 1968–1969.
1988–2015	Total return on benchmark 10-year Australian government bond, *Thomson Reuters Datastream*.

We are grateful to Josefin Meyer and Christoph Trebesch for sharing historical bond return data for Australia.

Belgium

Table A.17: *Data sources: equity and bond returns, Belgium*

Year	Data source
Equity returns:	
1870–2015	Total return on all common stocks of Belgian companies listed on the Brussels stock exchange, provided by Frans Buelens. Market capitalization weighted. See Annaert, Buelens, Cuyvers, De Ceuster, Deloof, and De Schepper (2011) for further details.
Bond returns:	
1870–1913	Total return on the 3% rente; price and yield data from Drappier (1937), Table II.
1914–1937	Data from the SCOB database shared by Frans Buelens; total return on long-term government bonds, aggregated from individual bond data.
1938–1995	Total return on long-term government bonds, from various issues of National Bank of Belgium *Economic Summaries* and Ten-year Statistics, calculated from monthly data. 1938–1953: 4% perpetual bonds. Spliced with the SCOB data over the period 1938–1940. 1954–1963: 5-20 year 4.5% bond issued before 1962; price changes estimated using movements in yields. 1963–1970: Weighted average of 5-20 year bonds issued before 1962 and 5+ year bonds issued after 1962. 1971–1989: 5+ year maturity bonds, price changes estimated from movements in yields. 1989–1995: basket of 6+ maturity bonds, mean maturity approximately 10 years, price changes estimated from movements in yields.
1996–2015	Total return on 10-year government bonds, National Bank of Belgium online database, price changes estimated from movements in yields.

We are grateful to Frans Buelens for sharing the historical equity and bond return series from the SCOB database of the Brussels stock exchange.

Denmark

Table A.18: *Data sources: equity and bond returns, Denmark*

Year	Data source
Equity returns:	
1893–1922	Weighted average of returns on individual shares, computed from price and dividend data in various issues of the statistical yearbooks (Statistisk aarbog, years 1896–1927). Weighted by 1926 share capital of the company where data are available, or by median share capital of the respective sector. From 1914 onwards, we use the official stock price index in the Statistisk aarbog, combined with dividend yields on individual shares.
1923–1999	Combination of dividend yields from Nielsen and Risager (2001) (market-cap weighted, circa 100 companies), and the share price index from Jordà, Schularick, and Taylor (2016), which is compiled from League of Nations, UN and IMF data.
2000–2015	Returns on the MSCI total return index, from *Thomson Reuters Datastream*.
Bond returns:	
1870–1990	Total return on long-term government bonds from Statistics Denmark (1969) and various issues of the Danmarks Nationalbank's *Monetary Review*. Perpetuals up to 1923, 10-40 year bonds for 1924–1980, 10-year maturity bonds from 1980 onwards.
1991–2015	Statistics Denmark, total return on the 10-year bullet loan

We are grateful to Kim Abildgren for helpful advice about the historical Danish stock return series.

Finland

Table A.19: *Data sources: equity and bond returns, Finland*

Year	Data source
Equity returns:	
1895–1912	Total return index from Poutvaara (1996), based on several banks.
1913–1990	Total return index from Nyberg and Vaihekoski (2014), from the data shared with us by Mika Vaihekoski.
1991–2015	HMX total return index
Bond returns:	
1870–1925	Total return on long-term Finnish government bonds listed abroad, constructed from individual bond data in Arola (2006) (data from the online appendix of Nyberg and Vaihekoski (2011)).
1926–1991	Total return on approximately 5-year maturity government bonds from Nyberg and Vaihekoski (2011), using price movements implied by changes in market yield.
1992–2016	Total return on the 10-year benchmark local currency government bond, *Thomson Reuters Datastream*.

We are grateful to Mika Vaihekoski for sharing data and assisting with numerous queries regarding the Finnish stock and bond return series.

France

Table A.20: *Data sources: equity and bond returns, France*

Year	Data source
Equity returns:	
1870–2010	Total return index from Le Bris and Hautcoeur (2010). Index constructed to mirror the methodology of the CAC-40: returns on largest 40 listed French firms weighted by market cap, with a continuously updated sample, market cap weighted.
2011–2015	Total return on the CAC-40 index.
Bond returns:	
1870–1969	Total return on 4% and 5% rente (perpetual bonds). Data provided by David LeBris, from Le Bris and Hautcoeur (2010).
1970–2015	Total return on a representative basket of long-term government bonds. Assume 10-year maturity before 1990 and 30-year after; as in Le Bris and Hautcoeur (2010). Price movements estimated from changes in yields at monthly frequency. Data provided by David LeBris, from Le Bris and Hautcoeur (2010).

We are grateful to David Le Bris for sharing data, assisting with numerous queries and providing helpful comments on the paper.

Germany

Table A.21: *Data sources: equity and bond returns, Germany*

Year	Data source
Equity returns:	
1870–1913	All-share value-weighted performance index from Weigt (2005) and Eube (1998).
1914–1959	Total return on the value-weighted top-30 blue-chip index from Ronge (2002).
1960–1990	Total return index from Gielen (1994), value-weighted, broad coverage. We use the "net" performance index, which excludes the adjustment for dividend income tax credit.
1991–1995	Total return on the DAX index.
1996–2016	Total return on the CDAX index.
Bond returns:	
1870–1903	Total return on listed long-term government bonds, arithmetic average of returns on individual bonds, with price and yield data collected from Homburger (1905) For early years we use regional bonds to fill gaps.
1904–1930	Total return on listed government bonds from the *Berliner Börsenzeitung*. Arithmetic average of individual bond returns. Average maturity generally 5-15 years. No data for the hyperinflation period of 1923–25.
1931–1943	total return on 4.5–6% government bonds (6% until 1935, then converted to 4.5%), aggregated using individual bond data from Papadia and Schioppa (2016), Deutsche Bundesbank (1976) and *Statistisches Jahrbuch für das Deutsche Reich*, various issues. Spliced with the *Berliner Börsenzeitung* series over 1928–1930.
1948–1955	Total return on mortgage bonds (Pfandbriefe, 4% and 5% coupons, from Deutsche Bundesbank (1976) and *Statistisches Jahrbuch für die Bundesrepublik Deutschland*, various issues.
1956–1967	Total return on public bonds from Deutsche Bundesbank (1976), using an average of bond returns for different issue yields. For years where the sample composition changes we use the return implied by yield movements, otherwise we use actual price changes.
1969–2015	REX government bond total return index, Bundesbank database series BBK01.WU046A.

We are grateful to Ulrich Ronge for sharing data and assisting with a number of queries, and to Carsten Burhop for helpful advice. We would also like to thank Andrea Papadia for sharing data.

Italy

Table A.22: *Data sources: equity and bond returns, Italy*

Year	Data source
Equity returns:	
1870–1887	Capital gain + dividend return on stocks listed on the Genova stock exchange. Cacluated using indices in Da Pozzo and Felloni (1964), which are a book capital weighted average of returns on individual shares.
1888–1912	Total return on shares listed at the Milan Stock Exchange from Baia Curioni (2001). Market cap weighted.
1913–1954	Capital gain + dividend return on a broad index of Italian shares from Rosania (1954). Market cap weighted.
1955–1969	Capital gain on a broad index of Italian shares from Mondani (1978) (capitalization-weighted), plus dividend returns computed using total dividends paid and market capitalization data (as total dividends in lira / market cap), covering the vast majority Italian listed firms. Data sourced from *Mediobanca: indici e dati*, various years.
1970–2015	Returns on the MSCI total return index, from *Thomson Reuters Datastream*.
Bond returns:	
1870–1913	Sum of lagged current yield and capital gain on the 5% perpetual bond (Rendita), computed from data in Bianchi (1979).
1913–1954	Sum of lagged current yield and capital gain on a representative basket of long-term government bonds, computed from data in Rosania (1954).
1955–1987	Total return on listed government bonds using data in various years of *Mediobanca: indici e dati*, targeting a maturity of 10 years. For the 1980s, only data on 3-5 year maturity bonds were used since longer dated government bonds were not typically listed on the stock exchange.
1988–2015	total return on Italian government bonds from a variety of *Thomson Reuters Datastream* indicies: *Merrill Lynch* Italian government, *Datastream* Italian government and 7-10 year Italian bond indices, and the *Datastream* Italy benchmark 10-year government bond index.

We are grateful to Stefano Battilossi for helpful advice about the historical series. We are also grateful to Massimo Caruso, Giuseppe Conte and Roberto Violi at Banca d'Italia for helpful advice and help in accessing historical publications.

Japan

Table A.23: *Data sources: equity and bond returns, Japan*

Year	Data source
Equity returns:	
1882–1940	Sum of capital gain (Laspeyres index, base 1934–36), dividend return and gain/loss from stock operations, weighted by clearing transaction volumes, from Fujino and Akiyama (1977).
1941–1945	Capital gain from Bank of Japan (1966) + dividend return estimated using 1940 dividend yield, growth in nominal dividends paid by Japanese businesses from Bank of Japan (1966), and share price growth from Bank of Japan (1966) (chain linked).
1946–1947	Stock exchange closed; no data.
1948	Capital gain from Unted Nations' *Monthly Bulletin of Statistics* + dividend return estimated using growth in nominal dividends paid by Japanese businesses, as above.
1949–1951	Capital gain from *Bureau of Statistics Japan*, Table 14-25-a "Transactions and Yields of Listed Stocks, Tokyo Stock Exchange 1st Section" + dividend return from Fujino and Akiyama (1977) + gain/loss from stock operations from Fujino and Akiyama (1977).
1952–2004	Capital gain and dividend return from *Bureau of Statistics Japan* Tables 14-25-a and Table 14-25-b, covering Tokyo Stock Exchange 1st and 2nd section, + gain/loss from stock operations from Fujino and Akiyama (1977) (note: the Fujino and Akiyama (1977) series stop in 1975).
2005–2015	Return on the MSCI total return index, from *Thomson Reuters Datastream*.
Bond returns:	
1880–1940	Lagged current yield + capital gain on central government bonds, from Fujino and Akiyama (1977). Price index used: Laspeyres, base 1934–36.
1941–1965	Secondary markets for government debt were shut down for a prolonged time after World War 2, hence we use government bond yield data (not total returns) for this period. Sources are Homer and Sylla (2005) for 1941–1963 (long-term government bond yield), and IMF's IFS database for 1964–65 (Section "Interest rates", Series "Government Bonds").
1966–1970	Lagged current yield + capital gain on central government bonds, from Fujino and Akiyama (1977). Price index used: Laspeyres, base 1969–71.
1971–1983	Total return on long-term government bonds; 9-10 year maturity, from Hamao (1991).
1984–2015	Total return on the Japanese 10-year benchmark government bond total, calculated from the index by *Thomson Reuters Datastream*.

We are grateful to Ryoji Koike for helpful advice, and to Yuzuru Kumon and Kaspar Zimmermann for assisting with collecting and interpreting the data.

Netherlands

Table A.24: *Data sources: equity and bond returns, Netherlands*

Year	Data source
Equity returns:	
1900–1995	Total stock return index from Eichholtz, Koedijk, and Otten (2000), based on a selection of Dutch stocks, using data kindly shared with us by Roger Otten. The stock exchange was closed from from August 1944 to April 1946, so the 1945 return covers the period August 1944–April 1946.
1996–2015	Return on the MSCI total return index, from *Thomson Reuters Datastream*.
Bond returns:	
1870–1900	Total return on the 2.5% perpetual bond, using data in Albers (2002).
1901–1987	Total return on long-term government bonds from Eichholtz, Koedijk, and Otten (2000), using data kindly shared with us by Roger Otten.
1988–2015	Total return on benchmark 10-year government bond, *Thomson Reuters Datastream*.

We are grateful to Roger Otten for sharing the data on historical stock and bond returns in the Netherlands.

Norway

Table A.25: *Data sources: equity and bond returns, Norway*

Year	Data source
Equity returns:	
1881–1914	Total return on all stocks listed on the Oslo stock exchange, market cap weighted. Constructed from share-level microdata collected from the following publications: *Kurslisten over Vaerdipapier* (the stock listing), *Farmand* magazine, and *Kierulfs haandbok over aktier og obligationer*, various years.
1915–2000	Capital gain from Klovland (2004b). Dividend return from various issues of Norway's historical statistics and statistical yearbooks (*Historisk Statistikk, Statistisk årbok* before 1970, and constructed from MSCI indices on *Thomson Reuters Datastream* after 1970, with the two series spliced over 1970–74. We compute the MSCI dividend return as the difference between the accumulation gain on the total return and share price indices.
2001–2015	Return on the MSCI total return index, from *Thomson Reuters Datastream*.
Bond returns:	
1870–1919	Total return on long-term government bonds listed on the Oslo Stock Exchange and major foreign exchanges. We use Oslo data unless there are few bonds being traded, in which case we rely on foreign exchanges. Oslo data come from *Kurslisten over Vaerdipapier, Farmand* magazine, and *Kierulfs haandbok over aktier og obligationer*. London data are from the *Investor Monthly Manual* (http://som.yale.edu/imm-issues), various issues. Other major markets' data are from Klovland (2004a), with price movements estimated from changes in yields.
1920–1992	Total return on 10-year government bonds, with price changes estimated from movements in monthly yields in Klovland (2004a).
1993–2015	Total return on benchmark 10-year government bond, *Thomson Reuters Datastream*.

We are grateful to Jan Tore Klovland for answering numerous queries and helpful advice, and to the staff at the Oslo Nasjonalbiblioteket for help in locating the historical data sources.

Portugal

Table A.26: *Data sources: equity and bond returns, Portugal*

Year	Data source
Equity returns:	
1870–1987	Total return on all shares listed on the Lisbon stock exchange, market capitalization weighted. Own calculations using share price, dividend and balance sheet information in the following publications: *Diario do Governo*, *Boletim da Bolsa* and annual reports of public companies, various years. For years 1900–1925, capital for a large number of companies had to be estimated using the trend in capital of a small number of firms. For year 1975, the stock exchange was closed because of the Carnation Revolution. We assumed no dividends were paid, and interpolated the stock prices of firms listed both before and after the closure to compute returns.
1988–2015	Return on the MSCI total return index, from *Thomson Reuters Datastream*.
Bond returns:	
1870–1993	Total return on central government bonds listed on the Lisbon stock exchange. Average maturity around 15–30 years. Computed from bond listings data in *Diario do Governo* and *Boletim da Bolsa*. Weighted by the capitalization of individual bonds. During 1975 the stock exchange was closed, and we used yield data from the Bank of Portugal Statistics, series "Yield on fixed rate treasury bonds—10 years (monthly average)", and estimated price movements from changes in yields.
1994–2015	Total return on benchmark 10-year government bond, *Thomson Reuters Datastream*.

We are grateful to Jose Rodrigues da Costa and Maria Eugenia Mata for help and advice in finding and interpreting the data sources for the historical Portuguese data. We are also grateful to staff at the Banco do Portugal archive for helpful advice and sharing data.

Spain

Table A.27: *Data sources: equity and bond returns, Spain*

Year	Data source
Equity returns:	
1900–1940	Total return on all Spanish ordinary shares listed at the Madrid Stock Exchange, weighted by market capitalization. Data for 1900–1926 were kindly shared with us by Lyndon Moore (see Moore, 2010a,b). Data for 1926–1936 were collected at the archive of the Banco de España, using stock exchange listings in various issues of the *Boletin de Cotization Oficial* of the Madrid stock exchange. The stock exchange was closed during the Spanish Civil war years 1937–1939. For these years, we calculated the returns using the average return on shares listed both before and after the exchange was closed, and assumed no dividends were paid (this seems reasonable since even in 1940, very few companies paid our dividends).
1940–1969	Historical IGBM total return index for the Madrid stock exchange from López, Carreras, and Tafunell (2005), Chapter 10, "Empresa y Bolsa", Table 10.33. All shares, market capitalization weighted.
1970–1987	Return on the MSCI total return index, from *Thomson Reuters Datastream*.
1988 - 2015	Return on the IGBM index from *Thomson Reuters Datastream*.
Bond returns:	
1900–1936	Total return on long-term government bonds listed on the Madrid Stock Exchange, market capitalization weighted, average maturity around 25 years. Data for 1900–1926 were kindly shared with us by Lyndon Moore (see Moore, 2010a,b).
1940– 1972	Total return on long-term government bonds from various issues of statistical bulletins, *Anuario Estadístico da España* (http://www.ine.es/inebaseweb/25687.do).
1973–1990	Total return on government bonds traded on the Barcelona stock exchange, from the *La Vanguardia* newspaper, various issues. Spliced with the series from statistical bulletins over years 1973–1975.
1989–2015	Total return on medium-term government bonds from various *Thomson Reuters Datastream* indices: medium-term government bonds, and benchmark 10-year government bond.

We are grateful to Lyndon Moore for sharing data and providing helpful advice. We would also like to thank Stefano Battilossi for help with locating the historical data sources, and staff at the Banco de España archive for assisting with our queries.

Sweden

Table A.28: *Data sources: equity and bond returns, Sweden*

Year	Data source
Equity returns:	
1871–2012	Total return index from Waldenström (2014).
2013–2015	SIXGX total return index, capitalization-weighted.
Bond returns:	
1870–1874	Total return on 4% and 5% perpetuals, using individual bond data in the online appendix of Waldenström (2014).
1874–2014	Holding period return on long-term government bonds from Waldenström (2014), generally targeting 10-year maturity.
2015	Total return on benchmark 10-year government bond, *Thomson Reuters Datastream*.

We are grateful to Daniel Waldenström for helpful advice regarding the historical Swedish returns data.

Switzerland

Table A.29: *Data sources: equity and bond returns, Switzerland*

Year	Data source
Equity returns:	
1900–1925	Total return on all Swiss stocks listed in Zurich, capitalization-weighted. Calculated using individual stock price and dividend data kindly shared with us by Lyndon Moore (see Moore, 2010a,b). The stock exchange closed from mid-1914 to mid-1916, and the 1915 return covers the period July 1914 to July 1916.
1926–1969	Total return on Swiss equities from Pictet and Cie (1998).
1970–2015	Return on the MSCI total return index, from *Thomson Reuters Datastream*.
Bond returns:	
1899–1926	Total return on all Swiss government bonds listed on the Zurich stock exchange, capitalization-weighted. Calculated using individual bond price and yield data kindly shared with us by Lyndon Moore (see Moore, 2010a,b).
1927–1984	Total return on Swiss bonds from Pictet and Cie (1998).
1985–2015	Total return on benchmark 10-year government bond, *Thomson Reuters Datastream*.

We are grateful to Lyndon Moore for sharing data and providing helpful advice, and to Rebekka Schefer for hepling us locate the historical sources.

United Kingdom

Table A.30: *Data sources: equity and bond returns, United Kingdom*

Year	Data source
Equity returns:	
1870–1928	Total return on all UK stocks listed on the London stock exchange, capitalization weighted, from Grossman (2002, 2015).
1929–1963	Blue-chip market capitalization weighted index based on the largest 30 stocks listed on the London stock exchange, from Barclays (2016).
1964–2015	FTSE all-share index, coving circa 98% of UK stocks' capitalization. Market capitalization weighted.
Bond returns:	
1870–1901	Total return on 3% and 2.75% consols from the *Statistical abstract for the UK*, various issues.
1902–1979	Total return on gilts (price change + lagged yield) from Barclays (2016).
1980–2015	Total return on benchmark 10-year government bond, *Thomson Reuters Datastream*.

We are grateful to Richard Grossman and John Turner for helpful advice regarding historical UK stock and bond return data.

United States

Table A.31: *Data sources: equity and bond returns, United States*

Year	Data source
Equity returns:	
1870–2015	Capital gain + dividend return from Shiller (2000) (up-to-date data from `http://www.econ.yale.edu/~shiller/data.htm`)
Bond returns:	
1870–1926	Total return on a basket of central government bonds around 10-year maturity. Calculated from prices of individual bonds in the *Commercial and Financial Chronicle*, various issues.
1927–1928	Total return on 10-year government bonds, price changes imputed from yields. Source: Aswath Damodaran database (`http://pages.stern.nyu.edu/~adamodar/New_Home_Page/datafile/histretSP.html`).
1929–2015	Total return on US long-term government bonds, from Barclays (2016).

We are grateful to Josefin Meyer for helpful advice concerning the historical bond return data for the US.

M. Taxes on real estate

Although the extent of real estate taxation varies widely across countries, real estate is taxed nearly everywhere in the developed world. International comparisons of housing taxation levels are, however, difficult since tax laws, tax rates, assessment rules vary over time and within countries. Typically, real estate is subject to four different kinds of taxes. First, in most countries, transfer taxes or stamp duties are levied when real estate is purchased. Second, in some cases capital gains from property sales are taxed. Often, the tax rates depend on the holding period. Third, income taxes typically also apply to rental income. Fourth, owners' of real estate may be subject to property taxes and/or wealth taxes where the tax is based upon the (assessed) value of the property.

This section briefly describes the current property tax regimes by country and provides estimates of the tax impact on real estate returns. With few exceptions, the tax impact on real estate returns can be considered to be less than 1 percentage point per annum.

Australia

Two kinds of property taxes exist. First, all but one Australian states/territories levy a land tax (no land tax is imposed in the Northern Territory). Typically, land tax is calculated by reference to the site value of the land (i.e. excluding buildings). Tax rates vary depending on the property value between 0.1% and 3.7%. Yet, the land tax is a narrow-based tax, i.e. many states apply substantial minimum thresholds and several land uses—such as owner-occupied housing—are exempt. Consequently, I will not consider any tax impact of land taxes on housing returns. Second, council rates are levied by local governments. Rates vary across localities rates and are set based on local budgetary requirements. Some councils base the tax on the assessed value of the land, others base it on the assessed value of the property as a whole (i.e. land and buildings) (Commonwealth of Australia, 2010). While all these specific make it difficult to determine an average or exemplary tax impact on returns, it can generally be considered to be well below 1%. Capital gains taxes apply only to investment properties, not to primary residences. Rates are higher the shorter the holding period. All Australian states levy stamp duties on property transfers. Rates vary across states and different types of property and may amount up to 6% of the property value (Commonwealth of Australia, 2010).

Belgium

Property taxes (*Onroerende voorheffing*) are levied on the cadastral value, i.e. the notional rental value, of the property. Rates range between 1.25% in Wallonia and Brussels and 2.5% in Flanders (Deloitte, 2016a). Using a tax rate 2.5% and a rent-price ratio of 0.045 (2012) the implied tax impact is $0.025 \times 0.045 \times 100 = 0.11\%$. Capital gains taxes of 16.5% are levied if the property has been owned for less than five years. Property transfer taxes amount to 12.5% of the property value in Wallonia and Brussels and 10% in Flanders (Deloitte, 2016a).

Denmark

Two kinds of property taxes exist. First, the national property tax (*Ejendomsvrdiskat*). The tax rate is 1% of the assessed property value if the property value is below DKK 3,040,000 and 3% above. The tax is not based on current assessed property values but on 2002 values. Second, a municipal land tax (*Grundskyld* or *Daekningsafgifter*) is levied on the land value. Rates vary across municipalities and range between 1.6% and 3.4% (Skatteministeriet, 2016). According to Pedersen and Isaksen (2015) the national property tax amounted to a little below 0.6% of property values in 2014 and municipal land taxes to about 0.07% giving us a combined tax impact of about 1.35% (Pedersen and Isaksen, 2015). No capital gains tax is payable if the property was the owners' principal residence. Stamp duties are levied on property transfers and amount to 0.6% of the purchase prices plus DKK 1,660.

Finland

Property taxes (*Kiinteistövero*) are levied by municipalities. Tax rates for permanent residences range between 0.37% and 0.8% of the taxable value where the taxable value is about 70% of the property's market value (KTI, 2015). The implied tax impact is therefore $0.8 \times 0.7 = 0.56\%$. Capital gains from property sales are taxed at progressive rates, from 30% to 33%. There is a 4% property transfer tax for property. First-time homebuyers are exempt from transfer taxes (KTI, 2015).

France

Property taxes (*taxe foncière sur les propriétés bâties*) are levied by municipalities. The tax base is the cadastral income, equal to 50% of the notional rental value (Public Finances Directorate General, 2015). Tax rates in 2014 ranged between 0.84% and 3.34% (OECD, 2016a). Using the rent-price ratio of 0.045 in 2012 and assuming a tax rate of 3.34%, the implied tax impact therefore is $0.045 \times 0.5 \times 0.034 \times 100 = 0.08\%$. Capital gains from property sales are taxed at 19%. Property transfer taxes amount to about 5% of the property value (Deloitte, 2015a).

Germany

Property laxes (*Grundsteuer*) are levied by federal states. Tax rates vary between 0.26% and 0.1% of the assessed value (*Einheitswert*) of the property and are multiplied by a municipal factor (*Hebesatz*). Since assessed values are based on historic values, they are significantly below market values. In 2010, assessed values were about 5% of market values (Wissenschaftlicher Beirat beim Bundesministerium der Finanzen, 2010). Municipal factors in 2015 ranged between 260% and 855% (median value of 470%) (Deutscher Industrie- und Handelskammertag, 2016). Using a tax rate of 0.5%, the implied tax impact is $0.05 \times 0.005 \times 4.7 = 0.12\%$. Capital gains from property sales are taxed if the property has been owned for less than 10 years (*Abgeltungssteuer*). Property transfer taxes are levied on the state level and range between 3.5% and 6.5% of the property value.

Japan

Two kinds of property taxes exist. First, a fixed assets tax is levied at the municipal level with rates ranging from 1.4 to 2.1 of the assessed taxable property value. The taxable property value is 33% of the total assessed property value for residential properties and 16% if the land plot is smaller than 200 sqm. Second, the city planning tax amounts to 0.3% of the assessed taxable property value. The taxable property value is 66% of the total assessed property value for residential properties and 33% if the land plot is smaller than 200 sqm (Ministry of Land, Infrastructure, Transport, and Tourism, 2016b). The implied tax impact is therefore $0.33 \times 2.1 + 0.66 \times 0.3 = 0.89\%$. Capital gains from property sales are taxed at 20% if the property has been owned for more than five years and at 39% if the property has been owned for less than five years. Owner-occupiers are given a deduction of JPY 30 mio. There is a national stamp duty (*Registered Licence Tax*) of 1% of the assessed property value and a prefectural real estate acquisition tax of 3% of the property value (Ministry of Land, Infrastructure, Transport, and Tourism, 2016a).

Netherlands

Property taxes (*Onroerendezaakbelasting*) are levied at the municipal level. Tax rates range between 0.0453% and 0.2636% (average of 0.1259%) of the assessed property value (*Waardering Onroerende Zaak (WOZ) value*) (Centrum voor Onderzoek van de Economie van de Lagere Overheden, 2016; Deloitte, 2016c). The tax impact on returns therefore ranges between about 0.05% and 0.26%. No capital gains tax is payable if the property was the owners' principal residence. Property transfer taxes amount to 2% of the property value (Deloitte, 2016c).

Norway

Property taxes are levied at the municipal level. Tax rates range between 0.2% and 0.7% of the tax value of the property. Typically, the tax value of a dwelling is about 25% of its assessed market value if the dwelling is the primary residence. Higher values apply for secondary residences. In addition, wealth taxes are levied at a rate of 0.85% (tax-free threshold is NOK 1.2 mio) on the tax value of the property (Norwegian Tax Administration, 2016). The implied tax impact therefore is $0.25 \times 0.7 + 0.25 \times 0.85 = 0.39\%$. Capital gains from the sale of real estate property are taxed as ordinary income at 27%. A stamp duty of 2.5% applies to the transfer of real property (Deloitte, 2016b).

Sweden

Property taxes (*kommunal fastighetsavgift*) are levied at the municipal level. For residential properties, the tax rate is 0.75% of the taxable property value with taxable values amounting to about 75% of the property's market value. Fees are reduced for newly built dwellings (Swedish Tax Agency, 2012). The implied tax impact is therefore $0.75 \times 0.75 = 0.56\%$. Capital gains from sales of private dwellings are taxed at a rate of 22%. Stamp duties amount to 1.5% of the property value (Swedish Tax Agency, 2012).

Switzerland

Most Swiss municipalities and some cantons levy property taxes (*Liegenschaftssteuer*) with rates varying across cantons between 0.2% and 3% (property taxes are not levied in the cantons Zurich, Schwyz, Glarus, Zug, Solothurn, Basel-Landschaft, and Aargau). The tax is levied on the estimated market value of the property (Deloitte, 2015b). The tax impact on returns therefore ranges between 0.2% and 3%. Capital gains from property sales are taxed in all Swiss cantons (*Grundstückgewinns-steuer*). Tax rates depend on the holding period and range from 30% (if the property is sold within 1 year) and 1% (if the property has been owned for more than 25 years) of the property value. In addition, almost all cantons levy property transfer taxes (*Handänderungssteuer*). Tax rates vary between 10% and 33% (ch.ch, 2016; Eidgenössische Steuerverwaltung, 2013).

United Kingdom

Property taxes (*Council tax*) are levied by local authorities. Each property is allocated to one of eight valuation bands based on its assessed capital value (as of 1 April 1991 in England and Scotland, 1 April 2003 in Wales). Taxes on properties in Band D (properties valued between GBP 68,001 and GBP 88,000 in 1991) amounted to GBP 1484 in 2015 (Department for Communities and Local Government, 2016). Since 1991, nominal house prices have increased by a factor of about 2.5. The implied tax impact in 2015 for a property valued at GBP 68,001 in 1991 is $1484/(68,001 \times 2.5) \times 100 = 0.87\%$.

No capital gains tax is payable if the property was the owners' principal residence. Property transfer tax rates (*Stamp Duty Land Tax*) depend on the value of the property sold and range between 0% (less than GBP 125,000) and 12.5% (more than GBP 1.5 m.) (Deloitte, 2016d).

United States

Property taxes in the U.S. are levied at the state level with rates varying across states and are deductible from federal income taxes. Generally, tax rates are about 1% of real estate values. Since property taxes are deductible from : and, while there is variation across states. Giglio, Maggiori, and Stroebel (2015) assume that the deductibility reflects a marginal U.S. federal income tax rate of 33%. The tax impact is therefore $(1 - 0.33) \times 0.01 = 0.67\%$. Property transfer taxes are levied at the state level and range between 0.01% and 3% of the property value (Federation of Tax Administrators, 2006).

REFERENCES

Abildgren, Kim. 2016. The National Wealth of Denmark 1845–2013 in a European Perspective. *Danish Journal of Economics* 154(1): 1–19.

Albers, Ronald Martin. 2002. *Machinery Investment and Economic Growth: The Dynamics of Dutch Development 1800–1913*. Aksant Academic Publishers.

Annaert, Jan, Buelens, Frans, Cuyvers, Ludo, De Ceuster, Marc, Deloof, Marc, and De Schepper, Ann. 2011. Are Blue Chip Stock Market Indices Good Proxies for All-Shares Market Indices? The Case of the Brussels Stock Exchange 1833–2005. *Financial History Review* 18(3): 277–308.

Arola, Mika. 2006. Foreign Capital and Finland: Central Government's First Period of Reliance on International Financial Markets 1862–1938. Bank of Finland Scientific Monograph E:37–2006.

Artola Blanco, Miguel, Bauluz, Luis E., and Martínez-Toledano, Clara. 2017. Wealth in Spain, 1900–2014: A Country of Two Lands. Working paper.

Australian Bureau of Statistics. 2014. Australian National Accounts: National Income, Expenditure and Product. Table 8: Household Final Consumption Expenditure. http://www.abs.gov.au/ AUSSTATS/abs@.nsf/Lookup/5206.0Main+Features1Dec%202013?OpenDocument.

Azevedo, Joao. 2016. *House Prices in Portugal, 1930 to 2015*. Master's thesis, University of Bonn.

Baia Curioni, Stefano. 2001. *Modernizzazione e Mercato. La Borsa di Milano Nella "Nuova Economia" Dell'et Giolittiana (1888–1914)*. Milan: EGEA.

Bank of Japan. 1966. Hundred-Year Statistics of the Japanese Economy .

Barclays. 2016. UK Equity and Gilt Study 2016.

Barro, Robert J. 2006. Rare Disasters and Asset Markets in the Twentieth Century. *Quarterly Journal of Economics* 121(3): 823–866.

Barro, Robert J, and Ursua, Jose F. 2008. Consumption Disasters in the Twentieth Century. *American Economic Review* 98(2): 58–63.

Bianchi, Bruno. 1979. Appendice Statistica: Il Rendimento del Consolidato dal 1862 al 1946. In *Capitale Industriale e Capitale Finanziaro: Il Caso Italiano. Bologna: Il Mulino.*

Birck, Laurits Vilhelm. 1912. *Ejendomsskatter Og Eijendomspriser: En Studie.* Copenhagen: G.E.C. Gad.

Bracke, Philippe. 2015. House Prices and Rents: Microevidence from a Matched Data Set in Central London. *Real Estate Economics* 43(2): 403–431.

Brailsford, Tim, Handley, John C., and Maheswaran, Krishnan. 2012. The Historical Equity Risk Premium in Australia: Post-GFC and 128 Years of Data. *Accounting and Finance* 52(1): 237–247.

Bureau of Economic Analysis. 2014. Personal Consumption Expenditures by Major Type of Product. `http://www.bea.gov/iTable/iTable.cfm?reqid=9&step=3&isuri=1&910=x&911=1&903=65&904=2011&905=2013&906=areqid=9&step=3&isuri=1&910=x&911=1&903=65&904=2011&905=2013&906=a.`

Butlin, N. G. 1985. Australian National Accounts 1788–1983. Source Papers in Economic History 6, Australian National University.

Cabinet Office. Government of Japan. 2012. Composition of Final Consumption Expenditure of Households Classified by Purpose. `http://www.esri.cao.go.jp/en/sna/data/kakuhou/files/2012/tables/24s13n_en.xls.`

Cairncross, Alexander K. 1975. *Home and Foreign Investment, 1870–1913: Studies in Capital Accumulation.* Clifton, N.J.: Augustus M. Kelley Publishers.

Cardoso, Abilio. 1983. *State Intervention in Housing in Portugal 1960–1980.* Ph.D. thesis, University of Reading.

Cardoso, Fátima, Farinha, Luísa, and Lameira, Rita. 2008. Household Wealth in Portugal: Revised Series. Banco de Portugal Occasional Papers 1-2008.

Centrum voor Onderzoek van de Economie van de Lagere Overheden. 2016. Tarievenoverzicht 2016. `http://www.coelo.nl/index.php/wat-betaal-ik-waar/tarievenoverzicht-2016.`

ch.ch. 2016. Besteuerung Von Immobilien. `https://www.ch.ch/de/besteuerung-immobilien/.`

Commonwealth of Australia. 2010. Australia's Future Tax System: Report to the Treasurer. `http://taxreview.treasury.gov.au.`

Da Pozzo, Mario, and Felloni, Giuseppe. 1964. *La Borsa Valori di Genova nel Secolo XIX.* ILTE.

Dagens Nyheter. 1892. Annonsering: 2 Stenhus Till Salu. *Dagens Nyheter* November 5, 1892.

Dagens Nyheter. 1897. Annonsering: Hus. *Dagens Nyheter* September 3, 1897.

Dagens Nyheter. 1899. Anonsering: Hrr Kapitalister. *Dagens Nyheter* December, 20, 1899.

Dahlman, Carl Johan, and Klevmarken, Anders. 1971. Private Consumption in Sweden, 1931–1975.

De Telegraaf. 1939. Stijgende Woningbouw in Ons Land. *De Telegraaf* (21): 47, January 21, 1939.

Deloitte. 2015a. Taxation and Investment in France 2015: Reach, Relevance, and Reliability. https://www2.deloitte.com/content/dam/Deloitte/global/Documents/Tax/dttl-tax-franceguide-2016.pdf.

Deloitte. 2015b. Taxation and Investment in Switzerland: Reach, Relevance, and Reliability. http://www2.deloitte.com/content/dam/Deloitte/global/Documents/Tax/dttl-tax-switzerlandguide-2015.pdf.

Deloitte. 2016a. Taxation and Investment in Belgium 2015: Reach, Relevance and Reliability. http://www2.deloitte.com/content/dam/Deloitte/global/Documents/Tax/dttl-tax-belgiumguide-2015.pdf.

Deloitte. 2016b. Taxation and Investment in Norway 2015: Reach, Relevance, and Reliability. http://www2.deloitte.com/content/dam/Deloitte/global/Documents/Tax/dttl-tax-norwayguide-2015.pdf.

Deloitte. 2016c. Taxation and Investment in the Netherlands: Reach, Relevance, and Reliability. https://www2.deloitte.com/content/dam/Deloitte/global/Documents/Tax/dttl-tax-netherlandsguide-2015.pdf.

Deloitte. 2016d. Taxation and Investment in United Kingdom 2015: Reach, Relevance, and Reliability. https://www2.deloitte.com/content/dam/Deloitte/global/Documents/Tax/dttl-tax-unitedkingdomguide-2015.pdf.

Department for Communities and Local Government. 2016. Council Tax Levels Set by Local Authorities in England 2015-16 (Revised). https://www.gov.uk/government/uploads/system/uploads/attachment_data/file/445085/150714_Revised_Council_Tax_Stats_Release_July_2015.pdf.

Deutsche Bundesbank. 1976. *Deutsches Geld-Und Bankwesen in Zahlen, 1876-1975*. Knapp.

Deutscher Industrie- und Handelskammertag. 2016. Realsteuer-Hebesätze. http://www.dihk.de/themenfelder/recht-steuern/steuern/finanz-und-haushaltspolitik/realsteuer-hebesaetze.

Drappier, Jean-Marie. 1937. La Conjoncture des Cours des Valeurs Mobilières, de Leurs Dividendes et des Taux dIntérêt en Belgique de 1830 à 1913. *Recherches Économiques de Louvain* 8(4): 391–449.

Edvinsson, Rodney. 2016. Historical National Accounts for Sweden 1800–2000.

Eichholtz, Piet M. A., Koedijk, C. G., and Otten, Roger. 2000. De Eeuw Van Het Aandeel. *Economisch-statistische berichten* 85.

Eidgenössische Steuerverwaltung. 2013. *Die Handänderungssteuer*. Bern: Eidgenössische Steuerverwaltung.

Eube, Steffen. 1998. *Der Aktienmarkt in Deutschland vor dem Ersten Weltkrieg: Eine Indexanalyse*. Frankfurt am Main: Knapp.

Federation of Tax Administrators. 2006. State Real Estate Transfer Taxes. http://statesbankruptcy.com/pdfs/State%20Real%20Estate%20Transfer%20Taxes.pdf.

Fox, Ryan, and Tulip, Peter. 2014. Is Housing Overvalued? RBA Research Discussion Paper 2014-06.

Fujino, Shozaburo, and Akiyama, Ryoko. 1977. *Security Prices and Rates of Interest in Japan: 1874–1975.* Tokyo: Hitotsubashi University.

Garland, John. M., and Goldsmith, Raymond W. 1959. The National Wealth of Australia. In *The Measurement of National Wealth*, edited by Goldsmith, Raymond W., and Saunders, Christopher, Income and Wealth Series VIII, pp. 323–364. Chicago, Ill.: Quadrangle Books.

Gielen, Gregor. 1994. *Können Aktienkurse Noch Steigen?: Langfristige Trendanalyse Des Deutschen Aktienmarktes.* Wiesbaden: Gabler-Verlag.

Giglio, Stefano, Maggiori, Matteo, and Stroebel, Johannes. 2015. Very Long-Run Discount Rates. *Quarterly Journal of Economics* 130(1): 1–53.

Goldsmith, R. W. 1962. *The National Wealth of the United States in the Postwar Period.* Princeton, N.J.: Princeton University Press.

Goldsmith, Raymond W. 1985. *Comparative National Balance Sheets: A Study of Twenty Countries, 1688–1978.* Chicago: University of Chicago Press.

Goldsmith, Raymond W., and Frijdal, A.C. 1975. Le Bilan National de la Belgique de 1948 à 1971. *Cahiers Economiques de Bruxelles* 66: 191–200.

Grebler, Leo, Blank, David M., and Winnick, Louis. 1956. *Capital Formation in Residential Real Estate: Trends and Prospects.* Princeton, N.J.: Princeton University Press.

Groote, Peter, Albers, Ronald, and De Jong, Herman. 1996. *A Standardised Time Series of the Stock of Fixed Capital in the Netherlands, 1900–1995.* Groningen Growth and Development Centre, Faculty of Economics, University of Groningen.

Grossman, Richard S. 2002. New Indices of British Equity Prices, 1870–1913. *Journal of Economic History* 62(1): 121–146.

Grossman, Richard S. 2015. Bloody Foreigners! Overseas Equity on the London Stock Exchange, 1869–1929. *Economic History Review* 68(2): 471–521.

Hamao, Yasushi. 1991. A Standard Data Base for the Analysis of Japanese Security Markets. *Journal of Business* 64(1): 87–102.

Hansen, Svend Aage. 1976. *Økonomisk Vækst I Danmark.* 6. Akademisk forlag.

Haynie, Henry. 1903. Paris Past and Present. *New York Times.* January 10, 1903.

Hjerppe, Riitta. 1989. *The Finnish Economy 1860–1985: Growth and Structural Change.* Studies on Finland's Economic Growth. Helsinki: Bank of Finland.

Hoffmann, Walther G. 1965. *Das Wachstum der Deutschen Wirtschaft seit der Mitte des 19. Jahrhunderts.* Berlin: Springer.

Homburger, Paul. 1905. *Die Entwicklung Des Zinsfusses in Deutschland Von 1870–1903.* Frankfurt am Main: Sauerländer.

Homer, Sidney, and Sylla, Richard E. 2005. *A History of Interest Rates.* Hoboken, N.J.: Wiley, 4th edition.

Istat. 2016. National Accounts, Final Consumption Expenditure of Households; Consumption of Fixed Capital by Industry. https://www.istat.it/en/national-accounts.

Jordà, Òscar, Schularick, Moritz, and Taylor, Alan M. 2016. Macrofinancial History and the New Business Cycle Facts. In *NBER Macroeconomics Annual 2016, Volume 31*, edited by Martin Eichenbaum, Jonathan A. Parker, pp. 213–263. Chicago, Ill.: University of Chicago Press.

Klovland, Jan Tore. 2004a. Bond Markets and Bond Yields in Norway 1820–2003. In *Historical Monetary Statistics for Norway 1819–2003. Norges Bank Occasional Paper No. 35*, edited by Øyvind Eitrheim, Jan T. Klovland, and Qvigstad, Jan F., chapter 4, pp. 99–181.

Klovland, Jan Tore. 2004b. Historical Stock Price Indices in Norway 1914–2003. In *Historical Monetary Statistics for Norway 1819–2003. Norges Bank Occasional Paper No. 35*, edited by Øyvind Eitrheim, Jan T. Klovland, and Qvigstad, Jan F., chapter 8, pp. 329–349.

Knoll, Katharina. 2016. As Volatile As Houses: House Prices and Fundamentals in Advanced Economies. Unpublished.

Knoll, Katharina, Schularick, Moritz, and Steger, Thomas Michael. 2017. No Price like Home: Global House Prices, 1870–2012. *American Economic Review* 107(2): 331–352.

KTI. 2015. The Finnish Property Market 2015. http://kti.fi/wp-content/uploads/KTI_FPM15_net1.pdf.

Kuvshinov, Dmitry, and Zimmermann, Kaspar. 2017. Going to the Market. Unpublished.

Le Bris, David. 2012. Wars, Inflation and Stock Market Returns in France, 1870–1945. *Financial History Review* 19(3): 337–361.

Le Bris, David, and Hautcoeur, Pierre-Cyrille. 2010. A Challenge to Triumphant Optimists? A Blue Chips Index for the Paris Stock Exchange, 1854–2007. *Financial History Review* 17(2): 141–183.

Leroy-Beaulieu, Paul. 1906. *L'Art de Placer et Gerer sa Fortune*. Paris: Librairie Ch. Delagrave.

Limburgsch Dagblaad. 1935. Advertentie: Steenen Devalueeren Niet. *Limburgsch Dagblaad* (222): 18, September 21, 1935.

López, Carlos Barciela, Carreras, Albert, and Tafunell, Xavier. 2005. *Estadísticas Históricas De España: Siglos XIX–XX*. Madrid: Fundacion BBVA.

Meyer, Josefin, Reinhart, Carmen C., and Trebesch, Christoph. 2015. 200 Years of Sovereign Haircuts and Bond Returns. Working paper.

Ministry of Land, Infrastructure, Transport, and Tourism. 2016a. Tax System on Acquisition of Land. http://tochi.mlit.go.jp/english/generalpage/4988.

Ministry of Land, Infrastructure, Transport, and Tourism. 2016b. Tax System on Possession of Land. http://tochi.mlit.go.jp/english/generalpage/4986.

Mitchell, B.R. 1988. *British Historical Statistics*. Cambridge: Cambridge University Press.

Mondani, A. 1978. Aspetti Metodologici dell'indagine Mediobanca Sullandamento dei Corsi e sul Movimento dei Capitali delle Società Quotate in Borsa Dal 1928 al 1977. *Risparmio* 1566–84.

Moore, Lyndon. 2010a. Financial Market Liquidity, Returns and Market Growth: Evidence from Bolsa and Börse, 1902–1925. *Financial History Review* 17(1): 73–98.

Moore, Lyndon. 2010b. World Financial Markets 1900–25. Working paper.

MSCI. 2016. Real Estate Analytics Portal. `https://realestateportal.ipd.com/#/`.

Nakamura, Emi, Steinsson, Jón, Barro, Robert, and Ursúa, José. 2013. Crises and Recoveries in an Empirical Model of Consumption Disasters. *American Economic Journal: Macroeconomics* 5(3): 35–74.

NERA Economic Consulting. 2015. Historical Estimates of the Market Risk Premium.

Nielsen, Steen, and Risager, Ole. 2001. Stock Returns and Bond Yields in Denmark, 1922–1999. *Scandinavian Economic History Review* 49(1): 63–82.

Nieuwe Tilburgsche Courant. 1934. Advertentie: Geldbelegging. *Nieuwe Tilburgsche Courant* (11946): 56, March 31, 1934.

Nieuwe Tilburgsche Courant. 1936. Advertentie: Geldbelegging. *Nieuwe Tilburgsche Courant* 58, August 14, 1936.

Norwegian Tax Administration. 2016. Municipal Property Tax. `http://www.skatteetaten.no/en/Person/Tax-Return/Topic-and-deductions/Housing/Municipal-property-tax-/`.

Nyberg, Peter M., and Vaihekoski, Mika. 2011. Descriptive Analysis of Finnish Equity, Bond and Money Market Returns. Bank of Finland Discussion Paper Series 14/2011.

Nyberg, Peter M., and Vaihekoski, Mika. 2014. Equity Premium in Finland and Long-Term Performance of the Finnish Equity and Money Markets. *Cliometrica* 8(2): 241–269.

OECD. 2016a. OECD Fiscal Decentralization Database: Recurrent Tax on Immovable Property. `http://www.oecd.org/tax/federalism/oecdfiscaldecentralisationdatabase.htm`.

OECD. 2016b. OECD Statistics. 5. Final Consumption Expenditure of Households. `https://stats.oecd.org/Index.aspx?DataSetCode=SNA_TABLE5`.

OECD. 2016c. OECD Statistics. Table 9B. Balance-Sheets for Non-Financial Assets. `http://stats.oecd.org/Index.aspx?DataSetCode=SNA_TABLE9B`.

Offer, Avner. 1981. *Property and Politics 1870–1914: Landownership, Law, Ideology, and Urban Development in England*. Cambridge: Cambridge University Press.

Papadia, Andrea, and Schioppa, Claudio A. 2016. Foreign Debt and Secondary Markets: The Case of Interwar Germany. Unpublished.

Pedersen, Erik, and Isaksen, Jacob. 2015. Recent Housing Market Trends. *Danmarks Nationalbank Monetary Review* (3): 51–62.

Peeters, Stef, Goossens, Martine, and Buyst, Erik. 2005. *Belgian National Income During the Interwar Period: Reconstruction of the Database*. Leuven: Leuven University Press.

Pictet and Cie. 1998. The Performance of Shares and Bonds in Switzerland: An Empirical Study Covering the Years Since 1925.

Piketty, Thomas, and Zucman, Gabriel. 2014. Capital is Back: Wealth-Income Ratios in Rich Countries 1700–2010. *Quarterly Journal of Economics* 129(3): 1255–1310.

Poullet, Gh. 2013. Real Estate Wealth by Institutional Sector. *NBB Economic Review* Spring 2013: 79–93.

Poutvaara, Panu. 1996. Pörssikurssien Kehitys Suomessa 1896–1929: Uudet Indeksisarjat Ja Niiden Tulkinta. Bank of Finland Discussion Paper.

Public Finances Directorate General. 2015. Overview of the French Tax System. http://www.impots.gouv.fr/portal/deploiement/p1/fichedescriptive_1006/fichedescriptive_1006.pdf.

Real, Werner Hermann. 1950. *Erfahrungen und Möglichkeiten bei der Aufstellung von Richtlinen für die Stadtplanung: Unter Besonderer Berücksichtigung der Verhältnisse in der Stadt Zürich.* Zürich: Eidgenössische Technische Hochschule.

Ronge, Ulrich. 2002. *Die Langfristige Rendite Deutscher Standardaktien: Konstruktion eines Historischen Aktienindex ab Ultimo 1870 bis Ultimo 1959.* Frankfurt am Main: Lang.

Rosania, L. 1954. Indice del Corso Secco e Rendimento dei Titoli Quotati in Borsa. *Banca d'Italia, Bollettino* 9: 539–71.

Saez, Emmanuel, and Zucman, Gabriel. 2016. Wealth Inequality in the United States Since 1913: Evidence from Capitalized Income Tax Data. *Quarterly Journal of Economics* 131(2): 519–578.

Sefton, James, and Weale, Martin. 1995. *Reconciliation of National Income and Expenditure: Balanced Estimates of National Income for the United Kingdom, 1920–1990*, volume 7. Cambridge: Cambridge University Press.

Shiller, Robert J. 2000. *Irrational Exuberance.* Princeton, N.J.: Princeton University Press.

Shinohara, Miyohei. 1967. *Estimates of Long-Term Economic Statistics of Japan Since 1868.* Volume 6: Personal Consumption Expenditure. Tokyo: Tokyo Keizai Shinposha.

Simonnet, François, Gallais-Hamonno, Georges, and Arbulu, Pedro. 1998. Un Siècle de Placement Immobilier. L'exemple de La Fourmi Immobilière. *Journal de la Société Française de Statistique* 139(2): 95–135.

Skatteministeriet. 2016. Ejendomsvaerdiskat og Ejendomsskat (grundskyld). http://www.skm.dk/aktuelt/temaer/boligskat-og-de-offentlige-ejendomsvurderinger/ejendomsvaerdiskat-og-ejendomsskat-grundskyld.

Stapledon, Nigel David. 2007. *Long Term Housing Prices in Australia and Some Economic Perspectives.* Ph.D. thesis, Australian School of Business at the University of New South Wales.

Statistics Belgium. 2013a. Final Consumption Expenditure of Households (P.3), Estimates at Current Prices. http://www.nbb.be/belgostat/PresentationLinker?Presentation=META&TableId=558000001&Lang=E&prop=treeview.

Statistics Belgium. 2013b. Huishoudbudgetonderzoek. http://statbel.fgov.be/nl/binaries/HBO%20uitgaven%20evolutie%201978-2010_nl_tcm325-167949.xls.

Statistics Belgium. 2015. Bouw en Industrie - Verkoop van Onroerende Goederen. http://statbel.fgov.be/nl/modules/publications/statistiques/economie/downloads/bouw_en_industrie_verkoop_onroerende_goederen.jsp.

Statistics Denmark. 1919. *Vurderingen til Ejendomsskyld Pr. 1 Juli 1916.* Number 10 in Statistisk Tabelvaerk, 5. Raekke, Litra E. Copenhagen: Bianco Lunoc Bogtrykkeri.

Statistics Denmark. 1923. *Vurderingen til Eijendomsskyld Pr. 1 Juli 1920.* Number 12 in Statistisk Tabelvaerk, 5. Raekke, Litra E. Copenhagen: Bianco Lunoc Bogtrykkeri.

Statistics Denmark. 1948. *Vurderingen til Grundskyld Og Ejendomsskyld Pr. 1 Oktober 1945.* Number 21 in Statistisk Tabelvaerk, 5. Raekke, Litra E. Copenhagen: Bianco Lunoc Bogtrykkeri.

Statistics Denmark. 1954. *Vurderingen til Grundskyld Og Ejendomsskyld Pr. 1 Oktober 1950.* Number 23 in Statistisk Tabelvaerk, 5. Raekke, Litra E. Copenhagen: Bianco Lunoc Bogtrykkeri.

Statistics Denmark. 1969. Kreditmarkedsstatistik. *Statistiske undersøgelser* 24.

Statistics Denmark. 2017a. Annual National Accounts. http://www.dst.dk/en/Statistik/emner/nationalregnskab-og-offentlige-finanser/aarligt-nationalregnskab.

Statistics Denmark. 2017b. Private Consumption (DKK Million) by Group of Consumption and Price Unit. http://www.statbank.dk/NAT05.

Statistics Finland. 1920. *The Republic of Finland: An Economic and Financial Survey.* Helsinki: Statistics Finland.

Statistics France. 2016a. National Accounts. 6.461 Consumption of Fixed Capital at Current Prices (Billions of Euros). https://www.insee.fr/en/statistiques/2839283?sommaire=2839395&q=consumption+of+fixed+capital#titre-bloc-63.

Statistics France. 2016b. National Accounts. Actual Final Consumption of Households by Purpose at Current Prices (Billions of Euros). https://www.insee.fr/en/statistiques/2387892?sommaire=2387999.

Statistics Germany. 2013. *Volkswirtschaftliche Gesamtrechnungen: Private Konsumausgaben Und Verfügbares Einkommen.* Beiheft zur Fachserie 18, 3. Vierteljahr 2013. Wiesbaden: Statistics Germany.

Statistics Netherlands. 1959. The Preparation of a National Balance Sheet: Experience in the Netherlands. In *The Measurement of National Wealth,* edited by Goldsmith, Raymond W., and Saunders, Christopher, Income and Wealth Series VIII, pp. 119–146. Chicago, Ill.: Quadrangle Books.

Statistics Norway. 1954. Nasjonalregnskap 1938 Og 1948–1953. https://www.ssb.no/a/histstat/nos/nos_xi_185.pdf.

Statistics Norway. 2014. Annual National Accounts. https://www.ssb.no/statistikkbanken/SelectVarVal/Define.asp?MainTable=NRKonsumHus&KortNavnWeb=nr&PLanguage=1&checked=true.

Statistics Switzerland. 2014. Haushaltungsrechnungen von Unselbstndigerwerbenden: Ausgabenstruktur nach Sozialklassen 1912-1988 (ausgewhlte Erhebungen). http://www.bfs.admin.ch/bfs/portal/de/index/dienstleistungen/history/01/00/20/01.html.

Swedish Tax Agency. 2012. Taxes in Sweden: An English Summary of the Tax Statistical Yearbook of Sweden. https://www.skatteverket.se/download/18.3684199413c956649b57c0a/1361442608341/10413.pdf.

Tarbuck, Edward Lance. 1938. *Handbook of House Property: A Popular and Practical Guide to the Purchase, Mortgage, Tenancy and Compulsory Sale of Houses and Land, Including Dilapidations and Fixtures; with Examples of All Kinds of Valuations, Information on Building and on the Right Use of Decorative Art.* London: Technical Press.

Tilly, Richard H. 1986. Wohnungsbauinvestitionen whrend des Urbanisierungsprozesses im Deutschen Reich, 1870–1913. In *Stadtwachstum, Industrialisierung, Sozialer Wandel: Beitrge zur Erforschung der Urbanisierung im 19. und 20. Jahrhundert,* edited by Teuteberg, H.-J., pp. 61–99. Berlin: Duncker and Humblot.

U.S. Census Bureau. 1942. *Statistical Abstract of the United States.* Washington, D.C.: US Government Printing Office.

U.S. Census Bureau. 2013. Census of Housing, Tables on Gross Rents and Home Values. https://www.census.gov/hhes/www/housing/census/histcensushsg.html.

Villa, Piere. 1994. *Un Siècle de Données Macro-Économiques.* Number 86-87 in INSEE résultats. Paris: INSEE.

Waldenström, Daniel. 2014. Swedish Stock and Bond Returns, 1856–2012. In *Historical Monetary and Financial Statistics for Sweden, Volume 2: House Prices, Stock Returns, National Accounts and the Riksbank Balance Sheet, 1860-2012,* edited by Rodney Edvinsson, Tor Jacobson, and Waldenström, Daniel, pp. 223–293. Stockholm: Sveriges Riksbank and Ekerlids förlag.

Waldenström, Daniel. 2017. Wealth-Income Ratios in a Small, Developing Economy: Sweden, 1810-2014. *Journal of Economic History* 77: 285–313.

Weigt, Anja. 2005. *Der Deutsche Kapitalmarkt Vor Dem Ersten Weltkrieg.* Frankfurt am Main: Knapp.

Whitehead, Christine, editor. 2012. *The Private Rented Sector in the New Century: A Comparative Approach.* Copenhagen: Boligokonimisk Videncenter.

Wissenschaftlicher Beirat beim Bundesministerium der Finanzen. 2010. Reform Der Grundsteuer: Stellungnahme Des Wissenschaftlichen Beirats Beim Bundesministerium Der Finanzen. https://www.bundesfinanzministerium.de/Content/DE/Standardartikel/Ministerium/Geschaeftsbereich/Wissenschaftlicher_Beirat/Gutachten_und_Stellungnahmen/Ausgewaehlte_Texte/2011-01-11-reform-der-grundsteuer-anl.pdf?__blob=publicationFile&v=3$.

West, and Partner. 2012. Immo-Monitoring 2012-1.

CPSIA information can be obtained
at www.ICGtesting.com
Printed in the USA
BVHW010738221119
564515BV00004B/43/P